Financing Health Care

Hilary Goodman and Catriona Waddington

UK and Ireland

A catalogue record for this book is available from the British Library

ISBN 0 85598 187 3

Published by Oxfam UK and Ireland
274 Banbury Road, Oxford OX2 7DZ
Designed and typeset by Oxfam Design 219/PK/93
Set in 10/12pt Times
Printed by Oxfam Print Unit on environment-friendly paper

Oxfam is a registered charity no. 202918

Contents

Acknowledgements   vi

Preface   vii

List of abbreviations   viii

Explanation of terms   viii

Chapter 1:   Introduction   1

1.1   What is health-care financing?   1

1.2   Why health-care financing is on the agenda   1

1.3   The politics of health financing   2

1.3.1 The evolution of health services in developing countries

1.3.2 The search for alternatives

1.4   Summary of contents   4

Chapter 2:   Financing health care: first thoughts   6

2.1   What needs to be financed?   6

2.2   Start with a real knowledge of your community   6

2.2.1 The local community

2.2.2 The national context

2.2.3 Household surveys

2.3   Beware of underestimating needs   8

2.4   Spreading the sources of finance   9

Chapter 3:   Methods of financing health care   11

3.1   Introduction   11

3.2.   Principal methods   11

3.2.1 User fees

3.2.2 Pre-payment (Insurance)

3.2.3 Direct transfers and grants

3.3   Other methods of financing health care   16

3.3.1 Voluntary work

3.3.1.1 Occasional voluntary labour

3.3.1.2 Voluntary health workers

3.3.2 Income generation

3.3.3 Occasional contributions and fundraising

3.4. Public financing   18

3.4.1 General taxation

3.4.2 Social insurance

3.4.3 Official development assistance

Chapter 4: Financing health care: what do we want to achieve?   21

4.1   What services are provided?   22

4.2   What incentives are created for user and provider?   23

4.2.1 User fees

4.2.2 Pre-payment schemes

4.3   Who uses the services, and who pays: is the programme equitable?   24

4.3.1 Who uses the services?

4.3.2 Who pays?

4.3.2.1 Programme support

4.3.2.2 Community support

4.4   Are sufficient resources raised?   29

4.4.1 What is sufficient?

4.4.2 How much is raised?

4.4.2.1 Cost recovery through fees

4.4.2.2 Pre-payment

4.5   Is there much waste and inefficiency?   32

4.6   What is the quality of health care provided?   34

4.7   Is the programme sustainable?   36

4.8   Are local people involved in planning and managing the health services?   37

4.9   What is the impact on other health providers?   38

Chapter 5: Dealing with practical issues   39

5.1   Estimating resource needs: creating a budget   39

5.1.1 Accounting for inflation

5.1.2 Contingency

5.1.3 Capital and recurrent costs

5.1.4 Foreign-exchange needs

5.1.5   Keeping notes on the budget

5.2   Setting prices for fees and insurance   42

5.3   Keeping accounts   43

5.3.1   Monitoring the accounts

5.4   Dealing with money: its handling, safe-keeping and control   45

5.4.1   Handling money

5.4.2   Safe-keeping of money

5.4.3   Supervision and control

5.5   Monitoring and evaluation   47

Chapter 6:   The rural health zone of Boga, Zaire   48

6.1   What services are provided?   49

6.2   What incentives are created for user and provider?   50

6.3   Who uses the services and who pays: is the programm equitable?   51

6.4   Are sufficient resources raised?   52

6.5   Is there much waste and inefficiency?   53

6.6   What is the quality of health care provided?   54

6.7   Is the programme sustainable?   55

6.8   Are local people involved in planning and managing the health services?   56

6.9   What is the impact on other health-care providers?   56

6.10 Conclusion   57

Appendix 1 The Bamako Initiative   58

Appendix 2 Household surveys and baseline information   60

Appendix 3 Threats to the sustainability of revolving drug funds   61

Appendix 4 Suppliers of low-cost drugs and equipment   62

Appendix 5 Steps towards rational prescribing and appropriate use of drugs   63

Appendix 6 Sample budget   65

Appendix 7 Setting prices   66

Appendix 8 Examples of cash book records   69

Appendix 9 Inputs for a health programme   71

Bibliography and further reading   72

Notes   75

Index   78

Acknowledgements

This is a product not just of our making. Very many other people have significantly contributed to this book. To the people whose labours have provided us with much material for illustrative examples and case studies, we are most grateful. They are Bernard François, Gimono Wamai, Jarl Chabot, Sue Chowdhury, Pat Nickson and Nyangoma Kabarole. A number of the same people, and also Lucy Gilson, have read successive drafts of the text and given supportive and constructive comments. Their contributions have been valuable in shaping the final product. Naturally, we hold the responsibility for any remaining errors, inconsistencies or unclarities.

Our thanks to Oxfam Health Unit for supporting this project throughout. Particular thanks to Claudia Garcia-Moreno and James Tumwine for their invaluable input, encouragement and patience.

Thank you to Pat Slater who continually transformed our rough drafts into beautiful documents. And finally, a word of appreciation to our families and friends who supported our work in many ways.

Hilary Goodman
Catriona Waddington

Preface

The aim of this book is to stimulate thinking and provide guidance on the issue of financing health care. It is intended principally for managers, health workers, and members of the community who are involved with non-government health programmes and who are facing decisions, for whatever reason, concerning the financing of all or part of the programme. However, it is anticipated that many other people with an interest in health-financing issues will also find it useful and informative. Although the text refers mainly to small projects and programmes, many of the same principles apply to larger-scale government health programmes.

The Guide suggests options, raises questions, and provides examples of ways in which health care can be financed. It does not suggest definitive solutions; nor does it recommend one method of financing as better than others. Instead, it aims to help readers think about what is best for their working situation. There are a number of reasons for this approach:

- Different methods of financing suit different situations. It is inappropriate to make a recommendation without an intimate knowledge of that situation, and a consideration of the relevant factors (e.g. needs, wants, constraints).

- It is unlikely that one single source or method of financing will be sufficient. It is common for programmes to operate using a variety of financing options.

- Any means of financing involves making compromises between conflicting objectives. Deciding which compromises are to be made should always involve widespread consultation between the users and providers of the health-care programme.

The Guide asks readers to consider which objectives are important to them, and which method of financing is most likely to meet those objectives. It is intended to be easily understandable to a wide audience and, as a Practical Guide, it concentrates on using examples from many parts of the world, illustrating different experiences of financing health care.

The Guide tries to avoid unnecessary jargon. However, at the beginning of the book there is a list of abbreviations and an explanation of terms, which should clarify any unfamiliar terms used.

List of Abbreviations

BELACD	Bureau d'Etudes et de Liaison d'Actions Caritatives et de Développement
CHW	community health worker
ECHO	Equipment to Charity Hospitals Overseas
GNP	Gross National Product
IDA	International Dispensary Association
IMF	International Monetary Fund
INRUD	International Network for the Rational Use of Drugs
NGO	non-governmental organisation
ODA	official development assistance
OECD	Organisation for Economic Co-operation and Development
ORS	oral rehydration solution
PHC	Primary Health Care
RDF	revolving drug fund
TBA	traditional birth attendant
UNICEF	United Nations Children's Fund
USAID	United States Agency for International Development
WHO	World Health Organisation

Explanation of terms

Capital items/ costs/ expenditure
Capital costs are incurred relatively infrequently. They tend to be associated with establishing an infrastructure, or setting up a programme. The costs of constructing buildings, and buying vehicles and equipment are examples of capital costs. Capital items are characterised by the fact that their use lasts over several years. For example, a computer is a piece of capital equipment, which will only need to be replaced after being used for a number of years. (See also *recurrent costs/items/ expenditure*.)

Cost recovery
The generation of income which will cover some or all of the costs of a programme. It usually refers to a situation where the community is contributing to the recovery of costs in some way, for example through a system of user-fees.

Cost sharing
This term is similar to cost recovery, and is sometimes preferred. It emphasises the importance of partnership and shared responsibility for the financing of a programme. Possible partners are individuals, communities, governments and NGOs.

Cross-subsidy

A cross-subsidy occurs when the money raised through selling one thing is used to subsidise the price of another, in other words, to keep its price down. In the context of selling drugs, a relatively cheap drug with the potential to raise money through a price mark-up could be used to cross-subsidise another more expensive drug, so that the price of that drug to the patient is below its cost price. The cross-subsidy is then partially financing the expensive drug.

Devaluation

The reduction in the official rate at which one currency is exchanged for another. For example, if $1 = 300 shillings, a devaluation could change this rate to $1 = 500 shillings. After the devaluation, each shilling is worth less in terms of dollars. In the absence of any other change, a devaluation will raise the price of imports on the domestic market and reduce the price of exports (to the overseas buyer).

Essential drugs

Priority drugs which are most needed in a given area. Taking into account the prime causes of mortality and morbidity in a region, an essential-drugs list will describe the most important drugs to procure. Use of the list will streamline the range of drugs which are purchased, stored and prescribed, and can contribute to improving the efficiency of drug use.

Exemption

If a patient is given an exemption, it means that he or she does not have to pay the charge which is normally levied on other patients.

Generic drugs

Pharmaceuticals described by their pharmacological names, rather than their brand names which are given them by the pharmaceutical manufacturers. The move to prescribe drugs by their generic name is part of the effort to save money, since generic drugs are much cheaper than brand-name drugs, and their use can reduce health service costs.

Inflation

A sustained rise in the general level of prices. The rate of inflation (the rate of increase in prices) is determined by a number of interacting economic factors.

International Monetary Fund

The primary function of the IMF (as originally established) is to provide short-term financial assistance to governments whose economies have a balance-of-payments deficit (i.e. who are importing more than they are exporting). Loans are made to cover the deficit, in the hope that this temporary relief will help the domestic economy back on the road to recovery. IMF loans are often associated with an insistence that governments implement economic stabilisation policies, which are short-term, immediate measures such as devaluation or the abandonment of state subsidies. The IMF is also beginning to use longer-term instruments, similar to those required in structural adjustment programmes.

Monetarism
A school of economic thought which argues that disturbances within the monetary sector are the principal causes of instability in the economy. It influenced the policies of Margaret Thatcher in the UK and Ronald Reagan in the US during the 1980s. A free-market approach with minimal government intervention in all aspects of economy and society would be consistent with monetarist thinking.

Non-governmental organisation
An organisation which is largely independent of government, and is usually non-profit-making. The term covers a wide range of different kinds of organisations, both small and large, national and international. NGOs play a significant role in health and development in many developing countries.

Payment-in-kind
Payment with goods or labour, rather than with cash.

Primary Health Care
Community-level health care. As well as providing basic, first-line curative care, PHC emphasises the importance of preventive and promotive health care, hence the importance given to such things as immunisation or family-planning programmes. PHC can also be described as a philosophy of health and health care which emphasises community involvement and equity as key principles.

Recurrent costs/items/expenditure
Costs which recur frequently, for items which need to be paid for regularly in order to maintain the operation of a programme (hence the alternative name, 'operating costs'). Staff salaries, costs of fuel and medical supplies, and rent payments are all examples of recurrent costs. Recurrent items are characterised by their short-term use, and their need to be replaced constantly. (See also *capital costs/item/expenditure*.)

Revolving drug fund (RDF)
A scheme whereby an initial sum of money is used to buy a bulk supply of drugs. The drugs are then sold to patients when they come for treatment, and the money paid by patients is collected and used to purchase a second supply of drugs when the first is depleted. Thus, the money 'revolves' around the system. Theoretically,

REFs are self-sustaining, and an attractive way of improving the drug supply using a one-time capital investment. However, there are many ways in which a RDF can break down and run out of money (become 'de-capitalised'). See Appendix 3 for more details.

Standard treatment guidelines
Guidelines which describe in detail a specific treatment schedule for a specific diagnosis. The guidelines are useful as a reference for health workers, and can support rational drug use and the improvement of prescribing habits.

Structural adjustment
A long-term programme or package of economic reforms advocated by the World Bank. An agreement by a government to undertake these reforms is often made a condition for its loans being sanctioned by the World Bank.

World Bank
The official name for the World Bank is the International Bank for Reconstruction and Development (IBRD), which describes its role as it was originally conceived in 1944. It was established to provide financial assistance for reconstruction in Europe following the second World War. Now its primary function is as a development institution, and it provides large, long-term loans to governments for development activities. It also provides technical assistance for development programmes.

1 Introduction

1.1 What is health-care financing?

'Health care financing' is a general term which refers to the resources used to provide health care. While it most often refers to money, it also includes other resources that are used, such as voluntary labour or gifts in kind (pieces of equipment, supplies). The issue of health financing relates to many aspects of health-care provision. While its prime concerns are how much money is used, how it is raised, how it is spent, and who controls it, the impact of these questions goes beyond mere matters of money. The means by which a health service is financed will have significant implications for the way it is run and the care it provides. The issue of health financing is therefore of much greater significance than might at first appear — in fact it is a fundamental issue in health-services delivery.

As an illustration of this point, take a situation where patients pay nothing to receive treatment, and health workers are provided with all the equipment and supplies they need to give high-quality care. Compare this with another situation where instead, patients have to pay the full (cost) price for all tests, materials, and drugs used in the course of their treatment. What differences might we expect to find in the two situations? We could reasonably expect that resources of all kinds (for example, time spent with health worker, number of tests performed, type and quantity of drugs used) were being used in very different ways. In the first situation, much less attention might be paid to the amount of drugs and supplies used, and health workers and patients may well use more than are really necessary. This has a bearing on the nature and quality of care being provided, as well as the level of patient satisfaction. Clearly, the way money is raised, and spent, directly affects service delivery.

1.2 Why health-care financing is on the agenda

Health-care financing is clearly an issue which *every* society that has some form of health care needs to consider. For example, the United States has, for many years, faced rapidly escalating health-care costs, and this has generated much debate on the nature of health financing and service delivery. The issue of financing health care and health services has received particular attention internationally in recent years. This has stemmed in part from the world economic decline during the 1980s, and the subsequent economic crises faced by so many countries, particularly those in the developing world.

Rates of economic growth slowed in the early 1980s as the world moved into recession. Oil prices rose, commodity prices fell, and the world-wide burden of debt — concentrated in developing countries — soared. With populations growing, rates of national income per head (GNP per capita) declined, and for some countries (notably in Sub-Saharan Africa) the rate of economic growth did not simply slow but went into reverse, and their economies actually contracted. With severe shortages of foreign exchange to buy imports, and competing claims on shrinking government budgets, health sectors worldwide faced tremendous resource cuts. With this situation little changed in the 1990s, the question of finding alternative means to finance health care therefore became an urgent and widely-debated topic.

1.3 The politics of health-care financing

1.3.1 The evolution of health services in developing countries

In many countries which gained their independence after the second World War, the colonial administration had established health services with the principal aim of protecting the health of the Europeans and of local civil servants and soldiers (in other words, those who were seen as important for the maintenance of the economic and political infrastructure). This generally meant that health services were only provided in the urban areas, along with a few public-health measures to protect against the communicable diseases which were most threatening to the colonists. The majority of the population used what they had always used for health care — herbs and traditional healers. They might also have had a limited access to mission hospitals which charged for their services.

At independence, ex-colonies wanted to extend their health services, many trying to emulate the systems which existed in the countries from whom they had become independent. Particularly in the case of ex-British colonies, this often meant ambitious plans to provide 'free' health care to their populations. Then, after 1978, when the Declaration of Alma Ata[1] was made, many governments took on the commitment of providing Primary Health Care. This meant spending additional resources on the creation of a system of health care which extended throughout the country to village level, relied less on hospitals and highly trained staff, and more on community health activities.

During the early- to mid-1980s, severe economic problems caused many governments to cut back on social spending, including expenditure on health care. It began to be very clear that in a great many countries, often already fragile health services were crumbling. Insufficient quantities of drugs and supplies reaching the places needing them; vehicles lying idle and buildings deteriorating for want of repair; health staff lacking motivation — these became common features of many health services. A number of factors (including political factors) contributed to situations such as these, but many of them clearly related directly to the issue of health-care finance — not only the resource shortage,[2] but also questions of efficiency and resource allocation.

1.3.2 The search for alternatives

Seeking alternative means to finance health services, contributors to a growing international debate looked both for new sources of finance and means of tapping into them. It was hoped that proposed changes would have a positive influence on the overall functioning of health services. The debate, however, became highly politicised, and it is easier to see how this happened if we first understand the international political context in which the debate began.

The 1980s saw a political shift to the right on the part of the major economic powers — it was the decade that saw the rise of Reaganism and Thatcherism and monetarist economic policies. The dominant political philosophy espoused policies of reduced government intervention in the economy, and the fostering of free markets, which meant that the private sector was encouraged to take on activities that had previously been the responsibility of governments. At the same time, many developing-country governments, crippled with debt and ailing economies, looked to the IMF and the World Bank for assistance. Governments were granted loans conditional on the implementation of economic stabilisation and structural adjustment policies. These policies were prescribed by the IMF and World Bank in an effort to return the domestic economies to a cycle of growth rather than decline. They often included (among other things) cutting imports, encouraging exports, reducing public expenditure (particularly in the social sectors such as health and education), and encouraging the private sector. In other words, the general World Bank policy framework was closely aligned with the free-market, non-interventionist approach.

The World Bank has had considerable influence in shaping national economic policies worldwide. The Bank published a policy document on financing health services in 1987,[3] which received much attention, and in its turn was influential in shaping domestic health policies. It advocated, among other things, that users of government health facilities be charged fees (such that the government could recover a proportion of its recurrent expenditure on health), and that private health-care providers be encouraged. This fuelled an increasing interest in the idea of cost recovery in health care, and clearly influenced the thinking behind the Bamako Initiative (see Appendix 1).

The discussion of health financing became polarised — fees and privatisation became associated with the political Right, and in response the Left shunned ideas concerning cost recovery. The Left tended to view user fees and increased commercialisation of health services with cynicism, arguing that it detracted from the idea of providing care according to need. Demanding that people should pay for health care was seen as increasing the burden of those most in need of care and least able to pay for it. A reluctance to consider alternatives to free health services became a barrier to the exploration of other means of health financing. However, the reality of the situation often was such that an insistence that health services should be free of charge meant that there would be virtually no health services at all. As for the Right, being convinced by the 'magic of the market', they often did not recognise the limitations and wider implications of charging fees and stimulating the private sector.

The matter of health-care financing has become coloured by political ideology, which can obscure the real issues. This Guide points to some of these real issues which, it is hoped, will better inform opinions of all kinds.

1.4 Summary of contents

Following this introduction to financing health care in Chapter 1, there are five more chapters. Chapter 2 introduces some 'first thoughts' when considering financing all or part of a programme. These are general ideas which will need to be followed up in more detail subsequently, but which are useful to bear in mind from the beginning. Before identifying what exactly needs to be financed, the health objectives and priorities have to be set. There is a caution also about the dangers of underestimating financial needs. Ideas can be gained from the community on the means of financing, and, finally, it is recommended that the programme should not rely on only one source of finance.

Chapter 3 outlines the principal methods of financing health care. These are fees, pre-payment (or insurance), and grants or transfers; an example for each of these methods is presented. Following this, some more unusual methods of financing are considered which can act as supplements to any of the above.

Any method of financing health care will have a bearing on the way a programme is run. Chapter 4 considers a number of questions to ask about this. They include 'What incentives are created for user and provider?'; 'Are sufficient resources raised?'; 'What is the quality of health care provided?'. The case studies introduced in Chapter 3 are discussed to illustrate the various points made.

Chapter 5 considers the practicalities of dealing with finances. Firstly it outlines how to create a budget which lays out specific financial requirements. Setting prices, keeping accounts, and handling money are other issues discussed in this chapter.

The final chapter presents a full case study of a health programme in Boga, Zaire, which for many years has been surviving on the user fees raised from the community. The questions raised in Chapter 4 are repeated and discussed in relation to this situation.

The Appendices provide more detailed information on a number of issues raised in the course of the text. A list of further recommended reading is given for those who wish to pursue the topic of health-care financing more fully.

2 Financing health care:
first thoughts

2.1 What needs to be financed?

One of the first questions to be asked about funding a health programme is 'Exactly *what* needs to be financed?' Before different financing alternatives are considered, it must be clear for which aspects of the programme funding is being sought. In order to identify the aspects of the programme which need funding, it is necessary first to specify the programme's priorities. The process of setting these priorities — who is involved and how they are decided — is an important question in itself, but the point being made here is that *health* priorities should set the agenda for *financing* priorities, not the other way round. The overall programme priorities (goals and objectives) should be established first. These will then set the framework for identifying the financial needs. Ultimately, financial needs will have to be very carefully specified in terms of the actual inputs required and their costs. This is dealt with in detail in Chapter 5.

2.2 Start with a real knowledge of your community

When thinking of ways to finance health care, it is important that the means being considered will be acceptable to the community, and will fit in with current social, cultural, political, and economic norms and practices. This means ensuring that proposals for a method of financing are sensitive both to the local situation and to the wider policies of financing health care in the national context. It is important therefore to know your community and to be aware of what practices or systems already exist — at the household and community levels — with regard to earning and spending money, and consuming health care.

2.2.1 The local community
If the community is largely a subsistence economy with few people earning cash, then it would be foolish to consider a method which relied wholly on immediate cash payments for health care. It is likely that there will be at least some cash in the economy, but you need to know what a typical family will normally have

access to. Cash availability is often seasonal, with families having more cash after harvest time. This implies that people will be more able to pay for health care at this time of year, and the method of financing should be designed to fit in with this. If there is cash available, do the women have access to it? You will also have to consider male-female relations, roles, and status, and how these influence the household economy and the control of family resources.

Looking at the ways in which people pay for or raise money for other things can give you ideas which you might follow. Is there any kind of community fundraising, and if so, how might you link in with it? In Guinea-Bissau there is a long tradition of households each contributing a certain sum once a year to a village fund. This is a way of saving communally for expensive occasions such as parties or funerals. When discussions began on how to finance a village health programme, it was decided to follow this tradition of pre-payment, and a health insurance scheme was started. (There are more details on this case in Chapters 3 and 4).

What can you learn from practices that already exist, about the problems and difficulties that people encounter when having to pay for goods and services? What kind of health care is available already, and how do people pay for it? Traditional healers often allow people to pay in kind or by doing service (for example by cultivating their crops), and sometimes do not charge people if they are not cured by their healing. How will this affect the willingness of the community to pay for other health services? Above all, involve people in the local community, and listen to their thoughts on developing a system of health financing.

2.2.2 The national context
Take a look also at how health care is financed nationally. What is the government involvement, and how do they fund it? How much responsibility falls to the consumer for payment, and what expectations on the part of the consumer has this already created? If the government provides free health care, then expecting payment from the community for the health care you are organising might meet some opposition. Knowing these things can help you formulate your own ideas, and gauge how well the health programme with which you are concerned is likely to fit into a wider context.

2.2.3 Household surveys
Eventually, very specific information about the community might be needed, in order to set price levels or to estimate how much money the community can provide. This kind of baseline information can be gathered from a household survey, where certain specific questions are put to a representative sample of households in the community. There is further information on household surveys and collecting baseline information in Appendix 2.

2.3 Beware of underestimating needs

The following example illustrates why it is important to think about the financing of all the items of a health programme.

BELACD (Bureau d'Etudes et de Liaison d'Actions Caritatives et de Développement) is a church-related NGO established in the Roman Catholic diocese of Pala in the south-west of Chad.[1] It supplies six first-contact health facilities with essential drugs. The philosophy of the programme is that the population should be 'financially autonomous', in other words, be able to continue the programme without reliance on external funding. Table 2.1, which shows how local, direct costs were shared between the community and a foreign NGO, gives the impression that the aim of financial autonomy was indeed being achieved as 97 per cent of local, direct costs were paid for by the community through user charges.[2]

Table 2.1: Cost-sharing of local, direct costs, BELACD programme, Pala, Chad, mid-1980s

Items	Community (%)	Foreign NGO (%)	Total (%)
Salaries	33	0	33
Drugs*	56	0	56
Transport for emergencies**	2	3	5
Miscellaneous***	6	0	6
Total	97	3	100

* Excludes vaccines.
** Original purchase cost, plus running costs (i.e. capital and recurrent costs).
*** Stationery, soap etc.

Certainly, the figure of 97 per cent in Table 2.1 seems impressive. But we need to look carefully at the table and ask some questions. What does 'local, direct costs' mean? Why is only transport for emergencies included? What about transport for supervisory visits? Is emergency transportation the only capital expenditure? Why are vaccines excluded from the drug expenditure, when they are surely a vital component of PHC?

The key to all these questions lies in the definitions of 'local' and 'direct'.

Expatriate salaries are excluded; so are supervision costs, including transportation and staff time. The programme involves a good deal of supervision, and regular teaching sessions on management issues. These activities are not included as direct costs. Equipment purchased outside Chad — such as equipment for the immunisation cold-chain — is also excluded. The recurrent costs of immunisations are excluded, partly because it is not felt appropriate to charge for immunisations and partly because it is an imposed priority, rather than a felt community need.

The table below shows a more complete costing of the BELACD programme.

Table 2.2: Cost-sharing in the BELACD programme, Pala, Chad, mid-1980s

Items	Community (%)	Government (%)	Foreign NGO(%)	Total (%)
Salary	18	0	29	47
Drugs	31	6	0	37
Transport*	1	<1	9	10
Equipment* & sundries	3	0	3	6
Total	53	6	41	100

* Original purchase cost, plus running costs (i.e. capital and recurrent costs).

From Table 2.2, we see that the community covers 53 per cent of the total cost of the programme through user charges.

The comparison between Tables 2.1 and 2.2 teaches a useful lesson — always consider *all* the components of a PHC programme when thinking about how to finance it. It is easy to over-estimate the percentage of costs which can be raised by user charges. It is also easy to be persuaded by information provided which does not quantify all the 'hidden' costs. Just looking at Table 2.1 might have led to the conclusion that the programme could manage without external support. In fact, sudden withdrawal of support would have been disastrous.

2.4 Spreading the sources of finance

The BELACD example in Tables 2.1 and 2.2 demonstrates that not all the components of a PHC programme have to be provided by the same people. For example, a government may provide staff, community members a building, and a non-governmental organisation some bicycles — all for the same PHC scheme. Once you have listed all the elements which need to be financed, different sources can be considered for different items or activities. Some NGOs, for example, prefer to provide capital goods such as vehicles and refrigerators. Many communities would prefer to fund drug costs or the maintenance of a local health centre, rather than evaluations or supervisory visits. The benefits of the latter may seem rather remote to community members.

Table 2.3 shows the distribution of finance amongst four providers in a programme in Indonesia.[3]

Table 2.3: Cost-sharing in a PHC programme, Indonesia, 1983-5

Programme	Government (%)	Community (%)	Church (%)	Foreign donors (%)	Total (%)
Education	2	< 1	6	16	24
Nutrition	< 1	7	< 1	2	9
Water & latrines	0	6	< 1	7	14
TBAs*	0	2	0	1	3
FP**	14	5	2	5	26
Immunisation	< 1	0	< 1	< 1	1
Tuberculosis	< 1	< 1	4	16	22
Treatment	0	< 1	< 1	< 1	1
TOTAL***	16	22	13	48	100

* Traditional birth attendants.
** Family planning.
*** Totals are rounded to the nearest percentage.

There were clear variations in the proportions provided by the different funding sources — over half of the nutrition and TBA programmes were financed by the community, whereas foreign donors provided more than 70 per cent of the finance for the tuberculosis control programme. The government's principal interest was obviously in family planning. The key to successful cost sharing is to decide which services are appropriate for which providers or sources of finance.

Sustainability can be increased by having many different funding sources, since this reduces dependency on any one source, and guards against the potential collapse of the programme if that source were to dry up. However, it must be remembered that it is also more demanding on the planning, co-ordinating and administrative skills of programme staff.

3 Methods of financing health care

3.1 Introduction

This chapter outlines a variety of methods of financing health care. It begins by briefly describing three of the principal methods:

- user fees
- pre-payment or insurance
- direct transfers and grants.

The three methods can be applied at different levels of the health system (primary, secondary or tertiary levels); involve different agents (government, NGO, community); and operate on different scales. These characteristics — the level, the agents involved and the size — will significantly influence the functioning of any one of these methods in practice. An example of each method is briefly outlined as illustration. (These will be elaborated in the next chapter.) The chapter then considers a number of other methods which are complementary to the principal financing method, namely voluntary work, income generation and occasional contributions and fundraising. It is not expected that any one of these methods of financing will be used in isolation; they will need to be mixed and balanced in the most appropriate way for the programme in question.

Although understanding government health-care financing is not the main focus of this book, it is important to have a knowledge of the principal ways in which money is raised publicly for financing health care. These are broadly outlined in the final section of this chapter.

3.2. Principal methods

3.2.1 User fees

The term 'user fee' relates to a charge made to the patient or user of the health service, for a treatment or service received. The fee might be for the consultation, drugs and dressings, diagnostic tests or all or any of these things. Fees are most commonly charged for curative services since people are generally more willing to pay for a 'cure' in the form of drugs or injections than they are for promotive or preventive services.

The structure of user fees for curative care can vary, but there are three common ways to design the fee structure for treatment.

1 The user is charged the *actual cost plus a percentage mark-up* of the drugs and dressings received.

For example, say the percentage mark-up was set at 150 per cent. If the drugs given to a child with malaria cost the health programme 10 Rupees, the fee would be

Fee = Cost plus (150% x Cost)

= 10 + (150% x 10)

= 25 Rupees

In this case the patient pays for exactly what is received, and there are no hidden subsidies in the price. This might be preferred by the patient. While the calculation here is straightforward, this system makes for quite a complicated administration since the price for each patient will be different. This has bearing on monitoring and supervision of money and drugs (see Chapter 5). Another disadvantage is that patients have no idea in advance what they will have to pay for their treatment.

2 The user is charged a *fixed fee for treatment* received. There are two ways of doing this:

the fee is the same for all diagnoses, or

diagnoses are categorised into a small number of groups, and each group has its own fee. Charging for different diagnostic groups allows for the fact that some conditions are much more costly to treat than others.

Under the first scheme, a patient with malaria would pay the same as a patient with pneumonia. With the second scheme, if malaria and pneumonia were in different diagnostic groups, the two patients would pay different fees.

This system is much simpler to administer since there are only a small number of possible fees to pay. It allows more expensive treatments to be subsidised by cheaper treatments — the higher cost is shared amongst the patients in general. The other side of this, of course, is that patients pay more than the cost for simple, cheap treatments. Prices can be publicised in advance.

However they are decided, treatment fees could be levied on their own, or in addition to a fixed fee for consultation.

3 The patient is charged a *fixed fee per episode of illness*. In this case, the user pays a fixed fee on the first visit and nothing further if subsequent visits (to the same health facility) relating to the original diagnosis are needed. As in the fixed fee system discussed above, the same fee might apply for all diagnoses, or different fees might relate to different diagnostic groupings. Additional fees might be charged for unforseen complications.

This charging method also allows for cross-subsidisation of treatments, and for prices to be displayed in advance. The added benefit is that it encourages people to complete the treatment, and to return to the health facility if there is no improvement in their condition.

All three types of user fee system could cater for price differentials for certain groups of people; for example, allowing for age or perhaps chronic conditions. Exemptions can be made altogether for the poor. The different systems of fee charging all have different implications for prescribing habits and rational use of drugs. This is discussed in Chapter 4.

Raising money through user fees is a method which has often been implemented in small-scale, locally-run projects. It is possible, however, to raise money this way on a larger scale, as is happening in a number of African countries, for example, where fees are now being charged at government health facilities. However, governments have usually only been able to recover a small percentage of recurrent health expenditures in this way.

Case study: User fees at Kasangati Health Centre, Uganda[1]

Kasangati Health Centre (KHC), a peri-urban facility situated just outside Kampala, had a history as a model health centre providing good-quality health care. Used as a teaching centre for the Institute of Public Health, it was also renowned for its research activities. However, during the 1970s it declined almost to the point of collapse, due to political and economic upheaval in the country. The health centre was finally rehabilitated with external support in the mid-1980s, but it was clear that a stable source of funding was needed to ensure its survival after donor support had been withdrawn.

In 1988 fees were introduced to supplement the government funding for the centre and to allow the continuation of the restored quality of service. Specifically, the money from fees was intended to be spent on three main areas: staff incentive payments, buying more drugs, and fuel for the vehicle. A uniform fee of 100 shillings per episode of illness was set for all curative services, regardless of patient-age, diagnosis or medication. Preventive health services remained free. Exemption from the fee was granted for children referred from the nutrition clinic, staff members and their families, and the poor. No person would be turned away because of their inability to pay — free treatment was available in such cases. This was well publicised by community health workers and through the Resistance Committee system.

13

The type of charge — a flat fee per episode of illness — was chosen for its administrative simplicity. The initial price was set by first estimating the costs (historical cost data was combined with projected costs of such items as staff incentive payments), and then dividing the figure by an estimated patient load (assuming a 10 per cent non-payment rate). The initial fee of 100 shillings was retained for a whole year despite escalating consumer prices. Then it was raised by 50 per cent, and again by 100 per cent ten months later.

The health centre and the community retained autonomy in planning, and administration of the funds collected. All the funds remained with the centre. It was planned that the income from fees would be spent mainly on three areas — incentive payments for staff (31 per cent); purchase of supplementary drugs (28 per cent); and fuel and vehicle maintenance (17 per cent). It was hoped that improving staff morale and attendance through incentive payments, plus increased drug availability, would improve the quality of patient care.

The advantages and problems from the Kasangati experience will be discussed further in Chapter 4.

3.2.2 Pre-payment (insurance)

Pre-payment schemes operate to provide health care only for people who are members of the scheme. In order to join, it is necessary to make a regular payment of a pre-determined sum, which means that people pay whether they are healthy or sick. This payment entitles a person to receive health care for little or no extra charge when they require it. It is really an insurance mechanism against the risk of falling ill and suddenly having to pay high treatment costs. A major advantage of pre-payment is that the costs of providing health care are shared between sick and healthy people. One significant difficulty with such a system is persuading people to join when they feel perfectly well.

Although all pre-payment schemes are based on these principles, the size of schemes and the way they are run differ considerably, depending on such factors as who is eligible to join, what health care is provided, and so on. For example, pre-payment schemes can be small, community-based schemes, or they can be run at the work-place for the benefit of employees. Social insurance, which operates at national level, is discussed in 3.4.2.

Case study: National community health insurance at village level, in Guinea Bissau[2]

The community insurance scheme in Guinea Bissau was established to pay for essential drugs at village level which were dispensed by the

Village Health Worker (VHW). What began in 1980 as a scheme adopted by a few villages, grew to become a national programme covering about 20 per cent of the population ten years later.

When the scheme was in its early stages, a village was given an initial six-month supply of drugs free of charge. Thereafter, the community (there were between 200 and 500 people in each village) collectively became responsible for deciding the amount and collecting the money to finance the continued supply. They had to allow for the fact that the monetary economy in rural areas was only slightly developed. Cash only circulated in villages following the harvest and was virtually non-existent for six months of the year. This clearly ruled out any direct payment of fees. There existed a long-established tradition in the community of fundraising for social events such as funerals, where people paid an agreed amount into a collective fund (called *abota*). It was decided to follow the same method of pre-payment to raise money to pay for the drugs.

Decisions about the scheme were made collectively in the village. The payment was made immediately after harvest, and the agreed size of the contribution grew from year to year. Seeing the value of an improved supply of drugs in the village, people became more willing to contribute an amount which ensured a year-long supply (this was equivalent to roughly a quarter of the price of a chicken from each person).

Each adult who paid the annual insurance contribution was given a receipt entitling the holder to free consultations and drugs, supplied by the VHW. A mother's receipt also entitled her children to free treatment. If someone who had not contributed fell ill, they were required to pay a lump sum greater than the original contribution. A breakthrough for the scheme came in 1983 when the Ministry of Health agreed to accept members referred by VHWs to government health facilities, at no extra cost (normally, a fee would have to be paid before receiving treatment at government facilities). The benefits of participating in the *abota* scheme encouraged more than 75 per cent of adults to join in most villages.

An advantage of the insurance scheme over a system of user-fees was its administrative simplicity. It would have been very difficult for a (largely illiterate) village health committee or supervising nurse to monitor and control incoming money. It was not difficult, however, to gather money in once a year, and to cross-check the amount collected with the number of receipts issued.

The advantages and problems from the Guinea Bissau experience will be discussed in Chapter 4.

3.2.3 Direct transfers and grants

Direct transfers and grants refer to the provision of a quantity of resources, whether money or supplies, which does not have to be repaid. The quantity of the transfer or grant will usually have been negotiated in advance, and it might be a regular payment or a one-off gift. Grants, in particular, are often made on the condition that they are utilised in a particular way, or that the money is spent on specific aspects of the health programme, as determined by the donor. An example of a direct transfer could be the Ministry of Health providing money for the salaries of health workers, or a supply of drugs, whereas an external donor agency might provide a capital grant for the purchase of vehicles.

3.3 Other methods of financing health care

It is unlikely that any single method of finance will meet all the needs of a health programme. Generally, there will have to be a mix and balance between different methods of financing. Described in this section are a number of other methods which can be used to supplement larger and more sustainable forms of health financing.

3.3.1 Voluntary work

Salaries are usually the most expensive component of a health programme. Labour which is provided free can substantially reduce the amount of money which needs to be raised. Voluntary work can be provided as needed in one-off contributions, or on a regular basis. However, it is important that there is sufficient motivation for people to give their time and energy without personal remuneration. Maintaining this motivation can become a problem. Demotivation is the most common reason why voluntary workers lose interest and withdraw their services.

3.3.1.1 Occasional voluntary labour

Human labour is often an abundant resource in communities, particularly during slack agricultural periods. Voluntary labour can contribute to health programmes in the form of construction or maintenance work. People are often willing to work unpaid if it is clear that something of benefit is being created for the community. Communities have frequently built their own health centres, laid water pipes, or dug latrines. In Boga, Zaire, the community built beds for the hospital.

3.3.1.2 Voluntary health workers

Many health programmes rely on the regular work of unsalaried Community Health Workers (CHWs). They provide basic routine health services, treating minor ailments, dispensing a small supply of drugs, and giving health education to their communities. Even though the CHWs are not salaried, the service they provide is not without cost to the health programme. CHWs must be trained, equipped, supervised and supported in order to be effective — all of these things cost money. Without the necessary supervision and support, CHWs can rapidly become demotivated and ineffective.

In some countries (in Ghana for example), poorly supported voluntary CHWs have been known to exaggerate their clinical abilities and advertise themselves as private 'doctors'. The programme in Guinea Bissau described earlier prevented this by training several CHWs in a village. This meant that no CHW could claim to hold 'secret' knowledge which could be sold to villagers. It also meant that the voluntary work did not take up too much of any one person's time.

Much has been written about the advantages and disadvantages of volunteer health workers. One author[3] observed that sustained voluntary CHW programmes — especially large-scale ones — are relatively rare. She attributed the high drop-out rates to the fact that the CHWs are not paid. They may earn a small, irregular income from drug sales or from gifts from their patients, but this alone is often not sufficient incentive for them to maintain an interest in their duties.

The high turnover often associated with the use of voluntary labour can be costly in terms of training provision, as there will be a recurrent need to train newly-recruited volunteers.

3.3.2 Income generation

Income generation is used here to mean earning income by ways other than by the principal methods described in 3.2. Sometimes the health component of a wider development programme may be funded by income generation from another component such as agriculture. Here are some examples of income-generating activities from around the world which have contributed to the financing of health services:

- running a bakery
- milling rice and other grains
- growing a palm plantation
- farming fish
- operating a printing press.

In a health programme, there are some possibilities for generating income, on a smaller scale. Listed below are a few suggestions:

- selling clean, used, disposable syringe barrels as hair curlers
- hiring out vehicles — expatriate consultants are often happy to rent vehicles
- using a word-processor to print out programmes, announcements etc.
- selling photocopies
- grazing goats on health centre land

- renting out tables and benches
- renting out health education equipment (puppets, video and film projectors) for entertainment purposes.

Some words of caution are needed about raising money by using health programme resources. Firstly, the funders of a piece of equipment must agree to its being used to raise money. Secondly, the routine work of the programme should not be disrupted by these activities. Thirdly, the charge for the use of programme equipment must be large enough to cover the extra wear and tear associated with the additional use. If this is not taken into account, the programme may find that it does not gain financially in the longer term, since equipment may need to be replaced sooner than it would under conditions of normal use.

Whatever kind of income-generating activity is used, it must be appropriate for the aims of the health programme. For example, it would be wholly inappropriate to raise funds through the sale of commercial baby-milks or expensive weaning foods.

3.3.3 Occasional contributions and fundraising

Communities can also generate resources for health care through occasional contributions of materials, cash or even land. Fundraising events such as festivals, dances, raffles or lotteries can also raise money. This kind of event tends to be more successful when the fundraising is for one specific, visible purpose. People prefer to raise money for a new item of equipment or repairs to a building, for example, rather than for ill-defined, general purposes.

3.4 Public financing

This Practical Guide is essentially orientated towards those who are seeking ideas on financing health care which they themselves can implement. It is therefore not the intention to discuss government financing at any great length. However, this chapter would not be complete without a brief mention of different methods of raising public money to finance health care, since government funds form a vitally important component of overall health finance.

3.4.1 General taxation

An important method of raising government revenues is through general taxation. In developing countries, the most important taxes are excise duties on imports and exports, sales taxes and business taxes. Income tax is less significant than in the developed world, as a smaller proportion of the workforce is in formal, paid employment. These taxes together go into the government treasury and are then allocated to different areas of public spending, only one of which is health. Clearly, the size of the government health budget depends both on the total resources available for public spending, and the relative priority given by the government to health (as opposed to other sectors such as education or defence). Due to the downturn in economic fortunes experienced in many developing countries, governments have been facing declining public expenditure budgets. Coupled with the fact that health is often low on the priority list of government spending, it becomes clear why in many countries, Ministry of Health budgets have been falling in real terms in recent years.

3.4.2 Social insurance

Another means of publicly financing health services is through social insurance (sometimes called *social security* or *compulsory health insurance*). This is a system which operates at national level, whereby people in formal, salaried employment make compulsory contributions of a certain percentage of their income, to the social insurance fund. Their employers and/or the government make additional contributions on their behalf, so the burden of payment is shared. From this source of finance, a health service is provided, often only for the people who contribute. It may be provided directly by the government, or alternatively, by another provider who will be reimbursed by the social insurance fund. The service would operate alongside any other publicly provided service which serves the population as a whole.

This means of providing health care is common in many countries of South America. There is much debate regarding the desirability of such a system. On the one hand it caters for the health-care needs of a section of the population. This means that the government can concentrate its resources on providing health services for the poorest who are not in employment. On the other hand it can create an inequitable two-tier health system — one which is well-resourced for the rich (employed), and one which is resource-poor for the rest of the population.

However, historically, it can be seen that nearly all countries which have achieved very high or complete health insurance coverage (in other words, countries which serve a large proportion of their population through services financed in this way), have gone through a transition stage of a compulsory health insurance scheme which initially was available only to that part of the population which contributed.[4] Therefore, the development of a social insurance scheme might be seen as an important precursor to a national health service which provides for all.

3.4.3 Official development assistance

Official development assistance (ODA) is now playing a larger role in government-financed health care. ODA, which goes directly to governments, incorporates both grants and non-commercial loans. It can either come from another government (bilateral aid), or from a multilateral donor such as the World Bank. Development banks also play a role in this. They are specialised financial institutions providing medium- and long-term loans for all kinds of industrial and social development, including health care. Government cut-backs in areas of social spending have given increased significance to ODA. The relative importance of this in total health sector spending differs enormously from country to country, but in certain instances it plays a very significant role. In Nepal for example, in 1990/91, it amounted to 22 per cent of total health care expenditure (excluding private out-of-pocket expenditure).[5]

4 Financing health care: what do we want to achieve?

The choice of financing methods will depend on what it is hoped to achieve with the health programme. Each method will have a different impact on a range of issues relating to service delivery. This chapter sets out nine questions to ask in relation to the health programme. The chapter will be most useful to you if you have in mind a particular method of financing, so that you can then use the questions to think about the advantages and disadvantages of that method. Ideally the questions should be asked not just at the planning stage, but also as part of regular programme monitoring. This is because many of the specific effects of the financing method cannot be predicted in advance and will only become apparent during implementation.

You are asked to consider such issues as service type and service quality, equity, efficiency, community participation and sustainability. The degree of importance that you give to any one question will vary. It will depend on your own viewpoint and the objectives of the health programme itself.

The questions are presented below. It is somewhat artificial to consider them each in isolation since many of the issues overlap with each other. The order in which they are listed is of no significance.

4.1 What services are provided?

4.2 What incentives are created for user and provider?

4.3 Who uses the services, and who pays: is the programme equitable?

4.4 Are sufficient resources raised?

4.5 Is there much waste and inefficiency?

4.6 What is the quality of health care provided?

4.7 Is the programme sustainable?

4.8 Are local people involved in planning and managing the health services?

4.9 What is the impact on other health providers?

The issues will be illustrated using the examples introduced in the previous chapter.

4.1 What services are provided?

This question asks you to assess the relative importance in the programme of curative services compared with preventive or promotive services. The answer can give some clues as to the suitability of any given method of financing.

People are much more willing to pay for medicines and curative services than they are for preventive or promotive care. This is not surprising, since curative care frequently offers an immediate solution to a visible problem. Drugs, particularly, are very popular in this respect — not only do they come in interesting, coloured capsules or tasty syrups, but they often also work with impressive speed. By contrast, it often takes time for individuals and communities to be convinced about the value of preventive activities. The connection between excreta disposal and rates of diarrhoea in children, for example, may not be readily apparent.

Curative services, and particularly the prescribing of drugs, have a potential for raising money from the community through charging, whereas preventive and promotive services generally do not. The danger then is that because of their money-raising potential, curative services can assume an even more exaggerated importance, to the neglect of the vital health promotion messages and preventive services of Primary Health Care.

How are non-curative activities financed? It is very difficult to find unusual examples of financing preventive and promotive health care — there is a need for more documentation of successful examples.[1] Generally, they are funded by government money or grants from donors who recognise that these important activities have little money-raising potential. They can also be cross-subsidised by another health-care activity which generates revenue. This was the case at Kasangati Health Centre in Uganda, where some of the income raised through fees for curative services was used to remunerate the Community Health Workers, thereby encouraging their work, both curative and preventive. Additionally, if there is a demand in the community for a particular preventive activity (e.g. the provision of latrines, or a vaccination campaign), the community may be willing to share the costs. In Kagando, Uganda, a small, voluntary charge was made for vaccination and for an antenatal care-service, which were provided through mobile clinics. The money collected covered the cost of fuel.

Even when Community Health Workers are paid and active, it is often the case that CHWs regard the curative aspects of their work as the most important, and preventive and promotive work as secondary. This is illustrated by a CHW from Ibanda (another part of Uganda), who, despite being very active in health education and home-visiting, said she had been unable to do any community-health work for two months due to the fact that her supply of chloroquine had run out. In other words, she abandoned *all* her duties because her drug supply had run low. Prevention of ill-health is easily overlooked and neglected.

If the provision of preventive activities is an objective in your health programme, you should consider whether the system of health financing will support or discourage this.

4.2 What incentives are created for user and provider?

Any method of financing will influence the delivery of health care by creating a set of incentives which are likely to guide the behaviour of all the players — both health-care providers and service users. Any financing method needs to be looked at critically in order to identify the incentives which are at work. Some will be positive incentives (incentives which work in your favour) and some negative incentives (ones which work *against* what you are trying to achieve). What incentives are at work in your programme, and what is their impact on the health of the users, and the health service itself? You may be surprised to find that the health programme is not altogether promoting healthy practice!

> In the UK, dentists used to be paid according to the treatment they carried out for their patients. It was often claimed that much unnecessary remedial work was undertaken and that many perfectly healthy teeth were being filled, and also that dentists did not take the time to give dental education or preventive advice to their patients. The clear financial incentive to the dentists was to do as much curative treatment as possible, with a questionable impact on the dental health of the population.

The issue of incentives is considered separately for user-fees and pre-payment schemes, below.

4.2.1 User fees
The type of fee will influence both the user's and the health worker's behaviour. If users pay a fixed fee per visit, then there will be an incentive for them to get their 'value for money'. This often means that patients make demands on health workers, putting pressure on them to give many different kinds of drugs or demanding injections instead of oral medicine. However, in satisfying the demands of the patient, the most appropriate treatment will not necessarily be given: the patient may not know what is best in health terms; it may also be inefficient for the programme as a whole, if what the patient demands is more costly than necessary.

At Kasangati, a flat fee was levied, and prescribing behaviour was strongly influenced in this way. There was found to be much over-prescribing — the prescription of drugs which are not medically necessary. Antibiotics were frequently given for gastro-enteritis, when simple oral rehydration solution (ORS) would have been sufficient, and injections in place of oral therapy.

If a charge per drug is made, the pressure on the health worker to over-prescribe is reduced, since the more drugs prescribed, the higher the charge to the patient. The difficulties of over-prescribing can be addressed by using an essential drugs list and standard treatment guidelines (see 4.5 below). Irrespective of financial issues, both these good practices should be encouraged in any Primary Health Care operation.

In the case of setting a fee per episode of illness, there is an intentional incentive for the user to visit the health facility as often as necessary to complete the treatment, at no extra charge.

4.2.2 Pre-payment schemes

A problem with pre-payment schemes is that once people have paid their annual membership fee, there is nothing to prevent them from 'over-using' the services available to them. In other words, they utilise them frequently and demand certain treatments, which is costly for the programme. To discourage this where it might become a problem, schemes often levy a small extra charge (called a co-payment) for each visit made to the health service.

In the case of Guinea Bissau this over-use did not seem to be a problem, partly because the village health workers held only a few, essential drugs so there was little room for making significant demands. Another important aspect of the scheme in Guinea Bissau was the fact that it allowed access at no further charge to other levels of the government health system, provided a referral had been made through the village health worker. This not only provided an incentive to join the scheme, but encouraged appropriate use of the health services, since people had an incentive to use the village level as the first point of contact.

4.3 Who uses the services and who pays — is the programme equitable?

Equity in the field of *health* ultimately concerns the distribution of 'health' within the population, and seeks to redress the inequalities whereby certain population groups are more healthy than others. In terms of *health services provision*, equity concerns the impact on health of the unequal distribution of resources for health care. The precise definition of the equity goal in health programmes is a matter of opinion, but as a principle concerning distributional fairness it is central to the philosophy of many NGOs.[2] It is also a cornerstone of the concept of Primary Health Care, which advocates the availability of relatively simple and cost-effective technologies for many, rather than sophisticated and expensive technology for a few privileged people.

To judge the impact of a particular form of financing on equity, it is necessary to consider who in the community benefits from health care and who pays for it. The essential element of evaluating the benefits and burdens of health care is an assessment of health care *utilisation* and *payment* in relation to socio-economic status — in other words, who uses and who pays?[3]

4.3.1 Who uses the services?

In order to address this question it is necessary to gather some data on utilisation, preferably data which can be broken down into groupings of interest such as age, sex, ethnic group, and socio-economic status. This is to provide answers to some of these questions:

- How many people use the services?   — How often?
                                        — Which services specifically?

- Who are they?   — What proportions are male and female?
                   — What are their ages?
                   — Which ethnic groups do they come from?
                   — What is their socio-economic status?
                   — Where do they live; nearby or far away?

- Are there some groups in the population who are over- or under-represented among the users of the health services?

This information can be recorded routinely or through special surveys at health facilities as people attend. Some information might have to be specifically sought through a household survey. After answering these questions you could then begin to ask *why* some people use the services and some do not. Are some people not coming because they cannot afford to, or because they prefer to use other forms of health care? Insight into this situation might allow you to make some changes in the way the services are operated.

In 1985, fees charged at government health facilities in Ghana increased substantially. In increasing the fees, the explicit aim of the government was to recover some costs from the community (previously only a nominal charge had been levied). In one region, Volta, this led to an immediate and rapid decline in out-patient numbers (see Figure 4.1). Although there was a small increase after the low of 1986, out-patient numbers had still not returned to their 1984 level by 1991. Utilisation in the rural facilities declined much more than in the urban ones, and the age group most affected was the 45s and over. Three common reasons given by people as to why they did not visit the government facilities were: lack of drugs; cost; rude or unhelpful staff.[4]

4.3.2 Who pays?

Who from the community pays for the services — how is the burden of payment shared? In the case of a pre-payment scheme, the burden of payment is shared by everyone who participates in the scheme, both sick and healthy, rich and poor. In this respect, the relatively healthy people who have less cause to use the services subsidise the services for those who need to use them often. If there were a sliding-scale payment which varied according to economic status, allowing the poor to pay less to join than the richer families, then in a similar way the rich would be subsidising the poor. Since it is often the poorer families who are most in need of health care, this system helps to reduce the inequalities of access to health care.

> Gonoshastya Kendra (GK) is a social development organisation in Bangladesh.[5] The health component of GK runs an insurance scheme which entitles members to subsidised curative care. One of the aims of GK is to concentrate on providing services for the poor, and so the fees for membership and clinic visits operate on a sliding scale. There are four groups, based on socio-economic status:
>
> **Group 1**: Families with no male earner or a disabled male earner. Membership costs 5 taka.
>
> **Group 2**: Families which cannot afford two meals per day throughout the year. Membership costs 10 taka.
>
> **Group 3**: Families which can afford two meals per day all year round, but which do not have a surplus. Membership costs 25 taka.
>
> **Group 4**: Families which have an agricultural or financial surplus. Membership costs 30 taka.

User fees, by contrast, raise money only from those who are already sick, so the burden is not shared. When people are sick is often the time that they are most vulnerable, and quite possibly short of money. There are a number of things that can be done, both by the programme and in the community, to support those who have difficulty in paying the fee.

Figure 4.1 Out-patients, Volta region

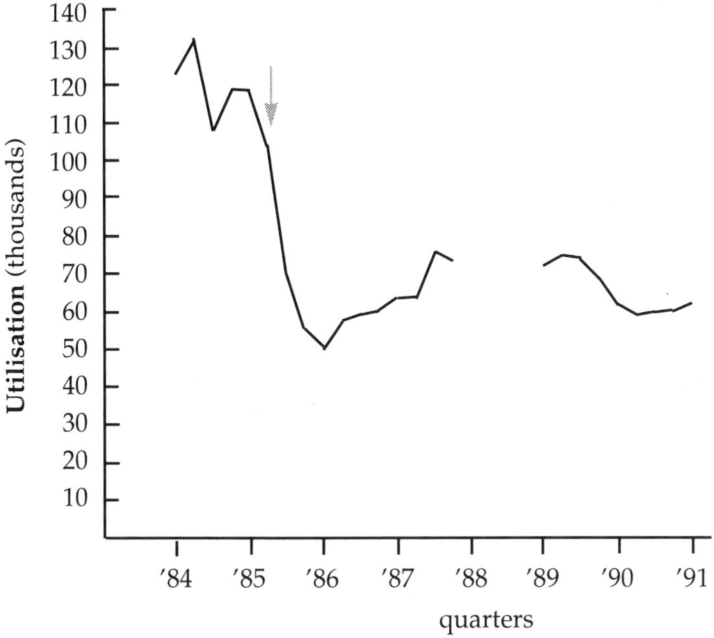

Arrow indicates fee increase. No data is available for the year 1988

Source: C Waddington (1992)[6]

4.3.2.1 Programme support

i Payment in kind, and credit: Accepting payment in kind — in the form of agricultural produce or labour for example — would assist those who did not have the cash available. (This only works if the payment in kind is directly useful to the health programme, or if the items can be sold for cash.) Allowing credit (repayment of the fees at a later date) is also a means by which the programme can assist those who do not readily have money. However, if this system is to work and the programme is not to lose money, there needs to be a mechanism by which debts can be followed up and recovered.

ii Exemptions: Giving exemptions from payment is another way of encouraging people who cannot afford the fee to attend the health facilities. Exemptions can be treatment-based — in other words, certain treatments such as those for TB and leprosy will be provided without charge in recognition of the high cost of treatment, and of the public health risks — or they can be offered to specific population groups, such as pregnant women or the poor.

In practice, there are often many problems associated with operating a system of exemptions. It helps first to decide clearly who should be exempt and then find a way of identifying them. Sometimes the decision over exemptions has been left to the discretion of health facility staff. This gives the staff a heavy burden of responsibility; can be humiliating for the people who come and have to be 'judged'; and lays the system open to much abuse. The power to recommend families for exemption from charges can rest with the village leader or village health committee, and this has worked well in some places, although there is also the risk of abuse of power. If a standard procedure for assessing the level of family wealth can be established (e.g. land-ownership or food availability throughout the year) the poorest families can be more clearly identified.[7]

Exemptions can sometimes discourage rather than promote equity, if those who are exempted are not the most needy. This is commonly seen where certain members of the population who are able to pay are exempt from paying, for example health staff and their families. Since the costs of treatment for these people must be recovered from elsewhere, it usually means that the burden of costs must now be spread across those who do pay the fees.

> At Kasangati, it was found that 80 per cent of non-paying patients were staff and their families. In other words, there were few disease-based or means-based exemptions given. Staff were also thought to have more influence over the type and quantity of drugs given out, so their treatment costs were likely to be higher than average.

Any policy of exemptions needs to be regularly monitored and reviewed to ensure that the exemptions are going to the intended people, and that the programme can sustain the financial costs of those exemptions (see 4.4 below).

4.3.2.2 Community support

There are also possibilities for community-organised support, such as loans or mutual savings clubs. Borrowing money from a money-lender can be very costly in the long run. A community loan scheme could instead offer loans at low or no interest, and favourable repayment conditions. A mutual savings club or 'tontine', as it is commonly known throughout francophone West Africa, is a scheme whereby each member of a group of people regularly pays a certain amount into a fund (e.g. each week). The fund is then drawn, say, once a month, and given to each member in turn, so that each person receives the fund once every few months. If there is some flexibility in the order in which people receive the money, unexpected expenses such as those incurred by health-care charges can be met more easily.

4.4 Are sufficient resources raised?

4.4.1 What is sufficient?

As was discussed in Chapter 2, it is easy to underestimate the costs of a health programme. Unsuccessful attempts have been made in the past to copy church-run health programmes which *appeared* to be wholly reliant on community financing (mainly through user fees). However, the outside observer might easily have overlooked the operational details of such church-run programmes. For example, significant costs such as salaries or vehicle costs might have been covered through donations from the local church, or from overseas. Health-worker salaries might have been low where people were working from a religious motivation rather than for a competitive salary. In other words, there are often hidden subsidies, and funding sources which are not easy to see. It is important for the sustainability of the programme that you are both realistic and clear about how much money (or what resources) you will need to raise. Once this has been established, it is then necessary to ensure as far as possible that any given mechanism will generate the required amount.

4.4.2 How much is raised?

When raising money for health care from the community, there is a trade-off between making the service accessible to people (charging money at a level they can afford) and raising enough money to provide services. Too much emphasis on fulfilling financial goals might lead to higher fees and fewer exemptions, which might in turn dissuade patients. On the other hand, liberal exemption and discount policies may improve access but also lose potential revenue needed to run the service. (Blakney et al. 1989.) This trade-off is evidenced in government health services in Ghana.

> In Volta Region, Ghana, community health nurses charge mothers a small fee for immunisations at their outreach clinics. Some mothers (it is not known how many) are deterred from bringing their children for immunisation because of the fee. However, the money raised pays for the health workers' transport to the clinic. In this way, immunisation coverage is extended since the immunisation fees allow them to hold more clinics than they would otherwise be able to.

The question to ask is: which are the priority goals, the health goals or the financial goals? Are there other ways of achieving the financial goals which might reduce the conflict between the two? The evidence of any trade-off can be identified through regular monitoring. Its effects can be alleviated by not relying too heavily on raising money from the community, but instead diversifying the sources of funding.

29

4.4.2.1 Cost-recovery through fees

Experience from around the world has shown that people are very often willing to pay for drugs, and that recovering drug costs, plus some additional costs, through drug and/or patient fees is possible. However, in a review of experiences in pharmaceutical cost recovery it was concluded that there is considerable variation in cost-recovery potential, and there is little basis for suggesting that large mark-ups of 100 to 200 per cent over costs are possible in most situations. This emphasises an important point, which is that the potential for raising money through fees of different kinds is *limited*, and that cost-recovery objectives have often been set unrealistically high.[8]

> At Kasangati, the objective of raising money through fees was to cover only some *supplementary* costs. The income derived was only a small percentage of total programme costs, illustrated by the fact that the cost of the basic drug supply alone was equivalent to roughly 85 per cent of fee income.

Take the example of drugs. The cost-recovery potential of charging for drugs depends broadly on two things. Firstly, it depends on the *costs*; secondly, it depends on the *'recovery potential'*, or the potential for raising money.

i Costs: total drug costs are determined by costs incurred in selecting, procuring, distributing and using the drugs. The programme managers will have some control over some of these costs (e.g. selection of drugs), whereas other costs incurred in this chain will be beyond their control. In some countries, rapid inflation or devaluation have the effect of raising costs, and this can present enormous problems for service providers. This issue is discussed more fully in Chapter 5.

ii Potential for raising money: this is the willingness and ability of people to spend their money at the health programme in question. This itself depends on many factors: the amount of money in the community (ability to pay), and the perceived value to individuals of utilising the health programme facilities, as opposed to seeking some alternative form of health care such as a traditional healer or private drug-seller (willingness to pay). If people are not willing to use your health programme because it takes hours to reach the health centre, or because they perceive the quality to be poor, then the recovery potential — the potential to raise money through fees — is diminished. This needs to be taken into account when setting prices (see Chapter 5 and Appendix 7).

The diagram opposite illustrates these points concerning cost-recovery potential.

Figure 4.2 Cost-recovery potential determined by patients and costs

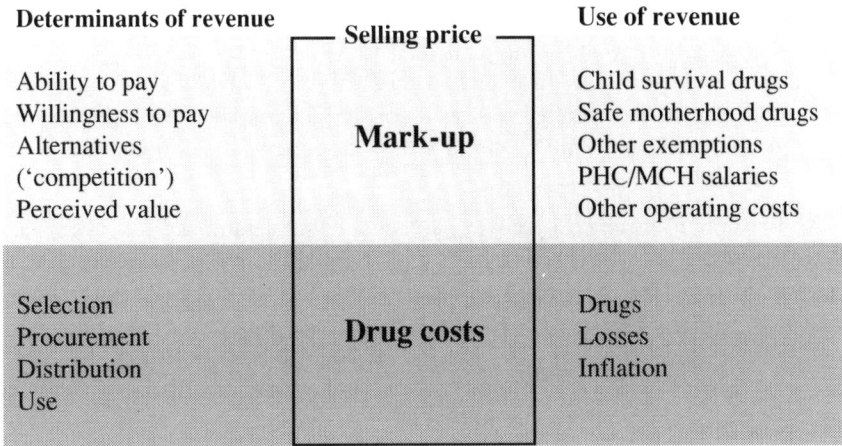

Source: Blakney et al (1989).

The experience at government facilities in most poor countries, in Africa at least, has been to yield averages of only around 5 per cent of recurrent costs through fees.[9] NGO and mission programmes have typically been able to raise more, since smaller programmes are probably more able to recover a higher percentage of their costs than larger ones. The Zairean example of Boga survived for many years almost exclusively through charging fees. The experience is described in detail in Chapter 6.

4.4.2.2 Pre-payment
One of the central issues relating to pre-payment schemes is that of raising sufficient resources through the membership fee to operate the desired health programme. A certain minimum number of people will need to be part of the scheme in order to raise enough money. Since people are much more used to paying for health services as they use them, the difficulty with a pre-payment scheme is often knowing how to encourage people to join the scheme even when they are healthy.

One way of doing this is to establish a financial incentive for people to join even when they are unsure whether they will use the services or not. A penalty, or higher membership charge, can be levied on those who only decide to join when they have already fallen sick and are in need of treatment. This was the case in Guinea Bissau.

Another way is to establish sufficient trust and confidence in the service delivery, so that people think it is worthwhile.

> In Guinea Bissau, to those people who argued that they rarely fell ill and saw little point in belonging to the scheme, it was pointed out that joining the *abota* scheme was a good protection for their children, who were more vulnerable to becoming ill than they were. Another significant incentive to join was the fact that membership allowed access at no further charge to other referral levels of the government health system. These measures were influential in achieving a participation rate of over 75 per cent in most villages.

An illustration of the cost-recovery potential being determined by patients and costs (see Figure 4.2 above) can also be found in the Guinea Bissau experience. It was the responsibility of each village to decide how much people should contribute to the collective fund. In the early years of the scheme, individual contributions were quite low, and insufficient to secure a drug supply for more than a few months. Slowly, as faith in the scheme grew, contributions increased until a year-long drug supply was purchased.

4.5 Is there much waste and inefficiency?

It is important to look critically at the programme and ask: are there any areas which are wasteful of resources? Are the available resources being put to maximum use? Could the same level and quality of service be provided at lower cost? If there are obvious areas of resource inefficiency then they are worth investigating to see if they can be improved. Otherwise, the implication is that money is being wasted, when it could be used to greater effect elsewhere in the programme.

Take the example of the cost of drugs to the health programme. This is determined by many factors such as the pattern of diseases in the area and drug selection; their purchase price; and the cost of transport and distribution. But since the gate-keepers to the drugs are the health workers who prescribe them, another significant influence on programme drug costs is prescribing behaviour.

> In Kasangati, prescription practices were monitored for some of the more common diagnoses. Notable findings showed that:
>
> - For malaria cases there was an increasing tendency to use injectable chloroquine, such that in 1990, 39 per cent of cases were treated in this way. This was due to patient demand and the belief of health workers that injections were a better form of therapy. Injections cost many times more than oral chloroquine.

- 55 per cent of patients were prescribed an antibiotic for cases of gastro-enteritis in addition to ORS. Prescribing unnecessary antibiotics is undesirable because of both the excessive cost, and the increased risk of drug resistance.

Inefficiencies relating to drug costs can be improved by a range of different activities, but two are particularly useful. Firstly, the use of an essential drugs list, and secondly, the use of standard treatment guidelines. These should, in any case, be basic components of Primary Health Care projects.

An essential drugs list will streamline the range of drugs which are selected and procured. This list matches the drugs purchased with the most common diseases in the area. It is generally only these most 'essential' drugs which are then ordered. This reduces the wastage of stocking the pharmacy with a large list of infrequently-used drugs. Ordering by the generic name of the drug is also cheaper than requesting brand names, and purchasing can be done through a number of organisations which sell generic drugs to non-profit making organisations at cost price (see Appendix 4 for details).

Standard treatment guidelines lay out detailed treatment information relating to specific diagnoses. For example, the standard treatment for an adult with pneumonia might be oral penicillin 250mg, four times a day for five days, plus ten analgesic tablets. The guidelines encourage appropriate prescribing practices and support the health worker in not giving in to patient demands. Effective use of these standard treatment protocols, however, requires training and regular supervision of health workers. It also requires regular monitoring of prescribing behaviour to guide the training and supervision. For more details on monitoring prescribing patterns see Appendix 5.

Another way of finding areas of waste is to ask in some detail how money is being spent, and whether actual expenditure matches budgeted or planned expenditure.

At Kasangati, expenditure of fee income for nearly two years was analysed. It was found that less money than planned was being spent on one of the principal purposes for which it was needed and intended, namely, buying supplementary drugs. More than expected was being spent on fuel and vehicle repairs, stationery and incidental expenses. Further questions were then required — was the budgeted expenditure unrealistic, or was money being spent unnecessarily on non-priority items instead of being used to buy drugs?

Table 4.1: Expenditure from Cost Recovery Funds, Kasangati: August 1988 - June 1990

	Health worker Incentive	PHC worker Incentive	Supplement-ary drugs	Fuel and vehicle repairs	Other staff allowances	Station-ery	Other
Planned %	31	5	28	17	10	0	9
Actual %	30	5	21	23	2	3	14

Another specific objective was to improve staff morale and reduce absenteeism by providing workers with an incentive payment to supplement their official salary. It became clear within the first year that staff absenteeism was unaffected by the payment, and yet it continued to be paid, using on average 30 per cent of money raised from fees.

How are the other resources being used? Is personnel time being used effectively, or are staff numbers and skills not well matched to the tasks that are required? Are patients treated at a higher level facility than necessary? Are other materials or supplies (e.g. fuel) used well? And are you gaining access to and making use of all the monies that are due to you, or are you not fully exploiting all the possibilities?

Many of these questions are essentially managerial issues, and can be highlighted through regular monitoring and supervision of all areas of the health programme. However, it may not be within the capacity of local management alone to change a situation for the better. For example, delays in delivering drugs and supplies might lie completely outside the influence of a programme manager. The challenge for management is to ensure that resources *within its control* are being used as efficiently as possible.

Decentralised management of the revenues raised for the health programme, and local autonomy over the expenditure of such revenues, provide a good incentive for careful cash collection and management. It has often been found that cost recovery is ineffective when the revenue is passed out of the control of local management and goes, for example, into a central Ministry or Treasury.[10]

4.6 What is the quality of health care provided?

The issue of quality of care concerns the performance of the whole service. It is not simply looking at outcomes and targets, but very much concerns the process and practices of service delivery. The issue is broad and touches on a number of areas already discussed in this chapter. For example, the effect of incentives on service provision was raised. Taking this further we can ask: how do incentives affect the quality of services? The entire range of activities in the health programme can be assessed for their contribution to the quality of service — e.g. the length of time and conditions in which patients wait to be seen, the skill of the health staff, and the availability of drugs.

Quality of care is a significant factor determining levels of utilisation — particularly *the quality as perceived by the user*. NGO health facilities which charge patients continue to be well-used even when services at nearby health facilities charge a lower fee or even nothing. This can be explained at least partly by the fact that users perceive the NGO facility to provide better quality care. In other words, the users' willingness to pay is in part dependent on the perceived quality of care delivered. This is important if attendance at a health facility is to be encouraged. It also clearly has bearing on the amount of money raised from patients whether through fees or pre-payment.

Studies investigating cost recovery in health programmes have found that people are often willing to pay for health care. They are much less willing however, to pay for services giving perceived poor quality care. Pharmaceutical cost-recovery programmes were investigated in a number of states in Nigeria, where there was a large decline in patient attendances associated with the introduction of fees. The decline was found to reverse only after the drug supply improved, in other words, when perceived quality had improved.[11]

Efforts at quality improvement are not always successful and it is essential to monitor any efforts so that improvements (or lack of them) can be identified. The example at Kasangati of the staff incentive payments is a case in point.

> The largest proportion of health centre fee-income was given to health workers as extra incentive payment, in an attempt to increase their motivation for attending work. When staff attendance did not increase significantly an investigation suggested that the payment was not high enough to make a difference. It was felt that a suitable rate of remuneration could not be generated from user-charges 'without raising the fee to a point that would significantly affect patient load or, without using almost all the collected money as staff incentive at the expense of other services'.

Quality improvements can be one-off actions (such as providing shelter for people to wait in) but most often they require follow-up. For example, the staff might be re-trained in the use of standard treatment guidelines. If, following training, there is no clear support to encourage good practice — such as regular supervision, or the monitoring of prescribing habits — then it cannot be guaranteed that the re-training will have its desired effect.

4.7 Is the programme sustainable?

Definitions of sustainability are many and varied, each emphasising different influences on the sustainability of a health programme.[12] They generally refer to the capacity of a system to survive in relation to a given level of external support. Sustainability does not necessarily imply self-sufficiency (depending solely on one's own strengths and resources). It does however, imply self-reliance, which describes a community's initiative in assuming responsibility for their own health development. A self-reliant community will know its own strengths and resources and know how to use them well. It will also understand its own limitations and know when and for what purpose to turn to others for support and co-operation.

Currently, a particular emphasis is given to the economic dimension of sustainability, where issues of financing play a dominant role. Many donor agencies have traditionally operated by providing only short-term support, in the hope that after an initial period, the programme will survive on its own. Recently, they have been questioning such policy and re-assessing the value of ongoing financial support. It is accepted now that longer-term support does not necessarily imply unsustainability, but is a recognition of the current economic constraints which many programmes face. Much of this book has emphasised the relevant issues when thinking about financial sustainability.

Many more factors influence the long-term sustainability of a health programme than simply its financial stability and security. The managerial and technical capacity in the programme is equally important, as is the external environment in which it operates. Programme sustainability may be threatened by unmotivated staff, or continuous currency devaluations. The issue of sustainability cannot be divorced from the political and economic climate surrounding a health programme, both in the local context, and in the wider national and international context (see 4.9). Some of the more common threats to the sustainability of revolving drug funds are shown in Appendix 3.

> Sustainability was a critical issue at Kasangati, and the establishment of user-fees was a mechanism aimed directly at contributing to the sustainability of the health centre.

> This is also a critical issue in Guinea Bissau where, unfortunately, the survival of the whole *abota* scheme is currently in question. Due to chronic theft and poor management at peripheral level, control over the scheme was centralised. This meant that the village had to make drug purchases from the capital city instead of the regional centres — a process which sometimes took more than a year. The communities justifiably became disillusioned with the scheme and stopped paying

membership fees. Though the sustainability of the *abota* scheme is therefore directly jeopardised by the fact that many people have stopped contributing, it is clear that the issue has deeper roots, which are linked to the management of the scheme. However, if the availability of reasonably-priced drugs returns to the periphery, there are hopes that *abota* can be revitalised.

While the economic viability of a programme might be the most visible indicator of its sustainability, the issue is intimately connected to many more factors than simply an ability to balance the books.

4.8 Are local people involved in planning and managing the health services?

The extent to which the community is involved with planning and management can significantly affect the operation of the health programme, and has a strong bearing on its sustainability. Community involvement is a determinant of a programme's acceptability in the community, and a determinant of the extent to which it fulfils community needs. However, a programme that has the blessing of the community is not guaranteed success, and likewise, one without its active support does not guarantee failure.

Community involvement can mean very different things, depending on the process by which decisions are made and the community representatives who are involved. On the one hand, planning and management can be fully consultative with a wide representation of the community. Or on the other hand, it can involve the community only in a nominal fashion. The characteristics of community involvement in any one setting will differ according to the community structures already in place. The successes and failures of community involvement will depend on the quality of commitment given to participation as a process — whether it is real, or whether it is a token gesture.

Sometimes community financing has been mistaken for community participation. But simply using community resources, whether money, goods or labour, does not in itself empower people to take responsibility for decisions which directly affect their lives. It is merely paying lip-service to something with which it has become fashionable to associate.

In the early years of the *abota* scheme in Guinea Bissau, it was left to each village to decide on the amount to be contributed by individuals. This was settled through a gradual process of learning how much people valued the supply of essential drugs, and discovering how much they

37

were willing to pay for them. Initially, a small contribution only bought enough drugs to last three months, and then there was a wait of another nine months (after the harvest) before more money was available to buy further drugs. Eventually, the size of the contribution people were prepared to pay increased to ensure a year-long supply of drugs.

Emphasising the *process of decision-making* is an important aspect of community participation. If the villagers in Guinea Bissau had known in the beginning the size of the contribution necessary for a year-long drug supply, many people would not have been willing to pay, either viewing the sum as too large, or resenting it as 'externally imposed'.

4.9 What is the impact on other health providers?

A health programme is unlikely to operate in a vacuum, separated from other forms of health care. There may be other agencies running similar services (government, private practitioners and NGOs); possibly private traders selling drugs and supplies; and almost certainly traditional healers. How does the programme affect these other health providers, both in the short- and the longer-term?

> Discussing a large revolving-fund for drugs in Khartoum, one NGO worker commented: 'Khartoum is a relatively rich city and has a flourishing trade in drugs on the private or semi-private market. If the revolving drug fund spreads and continues to provide drugs at well below market prices, we may drive these private traders out of business. We could do great damage if we caused this and then ceased to be able to continue to provide drugs. This is something that we must bear in mind, as well as being prepared for possible growing resentment from competitors.'[13]

It is not sufficient to be concerned solely with the operation of your own programme viewed in isolation, since its impact will be felt more widely. What are the consequences in a wider context of providing health care in this way? Is the programme undermining the efforts of another provider? Is it undermining the longer-term sustainability of health-care provision in the locality? Usually, NGOs have established health programmes in response to an unmet need in a given area. But putting money into high-quality care is not necessarily the most appropriate way in which to address the need, if such a programme stands alone. It may be competing with and outshining government services and in so doing, eroding the community's faith in government health care. This naturally has long-term implications for the sustainability of health care in the country as a whole.

5 Dealing with practical issues

5.1 Estimating your resource needs: creating a budget

Planning a programme involves making decisions about the overall goals (e.g. to reduce maternal mortality) and more specific objectives (e.g. to train 30 TBAs; to promote antenatal care) which the programme will aim to achieve. When it has been decided *how* these objectives will be met, the next step is to estimate resource needs by looking at *what* is necessary to run the programme in terms of staff, premises, equipment, supplies, and so on. In other words, a budget can be drawn up which outlines planned expenditure over a certain time period. If planned expenditure seems unrealistically high, you may need to reconsider the goals and objectives.

In order to produce a fully-costed budget for all or part of the programme, it is necessary first to itemise all the different inputs needed. It might be helpful sometimes to begin thinking in terms of the different activities (e.g. immunisation, health education, training, supervision) that take place, and then to break down each activity by listing the inputs required. Some examples of common inputs are given below.

(See also Appendix 9, p71).

Once all the inputs have been listed it is necessary to *quantify* them and finally to *estimate a cost* for each input:

- How many nurses are needed? What are their grades, and what will their salaries be? How much will be needed for their travel allowances to attend outreach clinics?

- How many bicycles are needed? How much will they cost?

- How much fuel will the vehicle use? How much will it cost?

Figures from last year may be available which record the quantities of inputs used (e.g. amount of diesel used by a vehicle), and these can be a useful guide for next year's estimates. If such figures are not available or appropriate, then make intelligent estimates based on whatever information is available. Estimates of costs may also be available from previous years (but remember to account for inflation — see below), and new estimates may need to be obtained from merchants or suppliers.

It might sometimes be appropriate to show in the budget the costs for a specific activity (which comprises many different inputs) as well as the costs for individual inputs. For example, if it is planned to run a three-day workshop to train TBAs, then it may be useful to show the *extra costs* specifically associated with the workshop. These might be: daily expenses for the trainers; food, accommodation and daily allowances for those attending; training materials. When drawing up a separate workshop budget, remember not to double-count (count twice) the cost of those inputs which are paid for as a matter of course in the programme, but which will also be used in the workshop (for example, rent for rooms, salaries for programme staff). This is why it was stressed that the extra costs alone should be added into the budget.

A useful hint about estimating future costs and resource needs is to be as realistic as possible. Do not skimp or make false economies in an attempt to keep planned costs down or something vitally important might be missed out of the programme. Similarly, do not exaggerate needs as this could result in setting a more difficult task than necessary in covering all the costs. Remember also that a budget is only an *estimate* of needs. Although it is desirable that the estimate should closely resemble the reality, adjustments to income or expenditure can be made later on if this does not turn out to be the case. (This is why monitoring the accounts is so important — see 5.3.1 below).

5.1.1 Accounting for inflation

Inflation is a rise in the general level of prices — it can be caused by many different factors in the economy. However, it is not the causes of inflation that concern us here as much as the effect. If the rate of inflation is 20 per cent, it means that, over the period of one year, general prices will increase by 20 per cent. If costs in the health programme rise at the same rate as inflation, the implication is that costs will rise by 20 per cent from one year to the next, even though the level of activity remains unchanged. This needs to be accounted for in drawing up a budget for the coming year.

Government offices dealing with economic planning make forecasts of the rate of inflation for the following year, and it may be possible to find out an estimate from them. If it is estimated that the annual rate of inflation is 20 per cent, then when estimating costs for the coming year, increase current prices by 20 per cent in the budget. The inflation rate for certain goods might be significantly greater than for others; for example, the prices of fuel and imported drugs might rise faster than locally-produced goods. If this is so, then adjust the planned fuel and drug costs accordingly. Often, health sector prices rise at a different rate from the rate of inflation. A common example is where salaries rise more slowly than general prices.

5.1.2 Contingency

Finally, when all programme costs have been estimated and added together, it is useful to add into the budget what is known as a *contingency allowance*. Since the budget is only an estimate of future costs it is quite likely that in some cases more money will be needed than was planned, due to unforseen circumstances (e.g. an epidemic), or to inaccurate estimation. It is therefore helpful to build some 'slack' into the budget, that is, some unallocated money which can be used for any eventuality. Different organisations allow for different contingency rates, but it is common to allow an extra 10 per cent of the total budget estimate as a contingency. Add this on to the total and this will give the total resource needs. (There is a sample budget in Appendix 6.)

When the budget estimate has been drawn up, it is useful to highlight two more specific aspects of the resource needs, namely *capital and recurrent costs*, and *foreign-exchange needs*.

5.1.3 Capital and recurrent costs

Capital items are characterised by the fact that the use made of them lasts over a number of years. They are replaced relatively infrequently (every few years). A vehicle is an example of a capital input; other examples are buildings, and certain expensive pieces of equipment such as computers. Capital items are very different from recurrent items, whose use is immediate and short-lived, and which need to be constantly replaced. Fuel for the vehicle is an example of a recurrent input (others are staff salaries, and drugs and medical supplies). Recurrent costs are also known as operating or running costs.

The size and frequency of the expenditure — and therefore the resource needs — for capital and recurrent items are very different, and it is useful to distinguish between the two kinds of costs in the budget. Since capital expenditures tend to be large, they can seem to distort the annual programme costs. For example, if a vehicle is bought in Year 1 of the programme, the total expenditure for that year would not necessarily represent the anticipated expenditure for Years 2 or 3 — the vehicle, which will not be bought every year, has exaggerated the annual costs. It is useful to make the capital costs stand out clearly in the budget.

5.1.4 Foreign-exchange needs

It is very important that the inputs which will have to be purchased with foreign exchange are identified in the budget. This is because special arrangements may be necessary in order to acquire the foreign exchange, and this needs to be planned for in advance. For example, if the programme is running a revolving drugs fund where the drugs are purchased directly from abroad, it is not sufficient to simply ensure that enough money is raised to cover the cost of new supplies of drugs, but an arrangement also needs to be set up whereby local currency can be exchanged for foreign currency. This is a problem for many programmes, since foreign exchange is usually a scarce resource which is not readily available. In some countries, it is difficult to convert local currency to foreign currency. Donors are sometimes able to help with this. In Boga, Zaire, the grant paid to the programme by a foreign donor was paid in hard currency into a bank account abroad, and this was used directly to purchase drugs.

It is common for the foreign-exchange needs of the programme to increase continually. Governments often use the exchange rate as a tool of economic policy, and the experience of many developing countries has been to witness the progressive devaluation of their currency. When a devaluation occurs it makes one unit of local currency *less valuable* in foreign-exchange terms than it was previously. For example, in 1990 the currency in Sierra Leone was devalued from a rate of $1 equal to 65 leones to $1 equal to 176 leones. In other words, the price of $100 worth of imported drugs changed suddenly from 6,500 leones to 17,600 leones! Devaluations can cause significant price increases overnight, so it is very important to be aware of how much of the programme's total costs are vulnerable to fluctuating exchange rates.

5.1.5 Keeping notes on the budget

A final word on drawing up budgets: it is very important to keep good notes stating the assumptions and original figures that underlie the budget calculations. If any of the expenditures need to be revised later on, such notes will make the task easier. It can sometimes be useful to write notes alongside the budget itself.

5.2 Setting prices for fees and insurance

Once it is established how much money needs to be raised, and how much is expected to come from the community in terms of fees or insurance, the next step is to calculate prices. How much needs to be charged in order to raise enough money?

Setting the right prices is not easy. Firstly, the calculations will be based not only on expectations and assumptions concerning costs, as was discussed above, but also on estimations of variables such as 'numbers of people attending' and 'numbers exempted'. Secondly, patient demand is in part determined by the price of health care, and the number of attenders might well vary depending on the price. To an extent, price-setting is a trial-and-error procedure, and prices can be adjusted from time to time as necessary. It is something that becomes a little easier with familiarity and experience in the programme.

When it has been decided which system of fee to use (cost plus standard mark-up, fixed fee for treatment, or fixed fee per episode of illness), calculations need to be made to estimate the appropriate fee structure. The framework for these calculations is outlined in Appendix 7.

5.3 Keeping accounts

A clear system of accounts facilitates good programme management. Accounts record the movement of money in and out of the programme — they therefore provide information concerning income, expenditure and available resources. Accounts are useful for *planning* purposes (when preparing a budget it can be useful to look back at past expenditure), for *monitoring and controlling* income and expenditure, and for *demonstrating* where the money has been spent (for purposes of accountability).

There are many different systems for keeping accounts, serving many different needs. Each organisation has its own preferences or rules concerning the accounting system. It is not possible here to go into detail about different methods of book-keeping, or present one method which caters for everyone's need and level of understanding. It is suggested that individuals follow this up for themselves as the need arises. The most basic concepts are, however, raised below.[1]

In order for the accounts to be kept accurately, make sure that every transaction or movement of money is written down. Wherever possible, get signed or stamped receipts as evidence of money coming in or going out. Compile the accounts, recording each transaction in an accounts book with one page for money coming in (income) and one for money going out (expenditure). Entries should be made regularly (daily or weekly) so that any errors can be detected early on and followed up. The current balance can always be calculated by subtracting the running total of expenditure from income: this should match the financial balance in reality (see example in Appendix 8). Check this regularly by comparing the calculated balance with the actual balance to make sure that no irregularities exist. Using bank, or financial, statements will help with this.

While adding up every single item of expenditure down to the last syringe is necessary to keep the records accurate, an accounts book with a large number of entries does not in this form provide particularly helpful information for planning or monitoring. It is much more useful to make an analysis of the accounts by grouping the entries, thereby eliminating unnecessary detail. Individual items could be grouped together under the headings that were made in the budget, so that 'bandages' and 'plasters' were both entered under 'medical supplies'. The accounts could be kept in this form from the beginning if this is thought to be helpful (see example in Appendix 8).

5.3.1 Monitoring the accounts

Monitoring is the process of comparing plans with actual performance, and so the accounts are monitored by comparing the financial plans (the budget) with what is actually happening. This is an important task, since the assumptions and estimates made in the budget could turn out to be wrong. By monitoring the accounts regularly (monthly or quarterly) to discover the difference between the plans and the reality, corrective action can be taken when necessary.

As an example, let us look at a programme which runs a revolving drug fund which aims to recover the total cost of drugs (including transportation and administration) through selling the drugs. It aims also to make a small surplus or 'profit' on the sale of the drugs, which will go towards funding materials for a women's income- generating scheme. It is expected that this will be approximately 500 dollars per quarter. A summary of the planned and actual performance for a three-month period is shown below:

	Actual	Planned	Difference (actual - planned)
Income (from sale of drugs)	7,000	5,500	1,500
Expenditure (cost of drugs)	6,750	5,000	1,750
Surplus (income minus expenditure)	250	500	250

Looking at these figures it is clear that although a surplus of 250 units has been made this quarter, it is not as much as was planned. There are many questions which could be asked in order to investigate why this was so.

Why is the income higher than anticipated? Is it due to unusually high attendance, or are people being prescribed more drugs than necessary?

Why is the expenditure so much higher than anticipated? Is it due to higher drug or transportation costs? Is there excessive loss due to expiry and poor drug management? Can all the drugs be accounted for — has there been any theft?

By asking these questions, it should be determined whether the difference between the actual and planned surplus was due to controllable factors or not. For example, unexpected price increases for drugs or fuel are not factors that the programme can control, whereas poor drug management can be addressed within the programme.

Can expenditure be controlled in such a way that the planned surplus is created for the income-generating scheme? If it cannot, then can income be increased by raising prices? If neither of these can happen, then perhaps the contribution to the scheme should be re-assessed if it looks unlikely that the drugs fund can be relied upon to support it.

Once some answers to these questions have been obtained, it may be necessary to adjust your planned figures for the next quarter-year or year, if by now having updated information you can identify likely under- or over-estimates in your original figures.

5.4 Dealing with money: its handling, safe-keeping and control

If the health programme is financing some of its activities by raising money from the community, clearly there need to be mechanisms to ensure that the correct amounts of money are collected, stored safely, and accounted for. Dealing with money is not always easy because of the temptations and suspicions that it creates. It is important that the procedures for handling and control have been well thought out and are regularly supervised and monitored to ensure their effectiveness. Losing money through theft or mismanagement could jeopardise the programme and sour community relations.

5.4.1 Handling money
If money is being collected in payment for health care, whether for drugs, consultations or anything else, it is important that records are made of the transactions. The patients paying should be given a receipt or some kind of proof of payment, and the money-collector should keep records of who has paid what. It should therefore be easy to add up the total amount collected in any one day. At the end of each day someone other than the money-collector should count the money and check that it tallies with the amount recorded on the collection-sheets.

As well as being able to check that the records match the amount collected, it is helpful for a supervisor to be able to cross-check the system of money collection. This might be done with information from another record system, perhaps attendances or prescriptions recorded by the medical assistants. A supervisor needs to be confident that the money-collector has accurately recorded all the money that has been paid. This is why it is of great benefit to have a simple method of payment and collection — the more complex a system, the more open it is to abuse and unintentional error.

Careful consideration should be given as to *who* should handle the money. For the people involved it often means handling money many times the value of their salaries (which may be paid irregularly and infrequently). For this reason alone, handling money becomes a temptation. Sometimes health staff are unwilling to perform this task, and a project in Mali selected and trained individuals from outside the project to be the money-collectors. They were paid out of the money collected from the drug fees, which brought an additional cost for the project to recover. However, the fact that these people were not government workers was a great advantage, because they could more easily be disciplined or fired in the event of mismanagement.[2]

5.4.2 Safe-keeping of money

Once money has been collected it must be kept safely. How this can best be done depends on the local situation. Banks or post offices are good places to deposit money regularly, if they are accessible. There may be an added advantage here if the bank is willing to pay interest on the deposits.

If it is not possible to keep money in a bank account, then a way of holding or using the money must be thought of. Is there a safe that can be used, or a cash box that can be securely locked away?

> In a health zone in Zaire, the money from health fees was kept by the village health committee in a box with two locks. The keys were held by different people, and three people were needed to oversee any withdrawal or deposit. Although such a system may seem rather cumbersome, it was the solution which the village committee came up with after a previous experience when the nurse had absconded with the funds.

Any person or premises known to be holding cash is vulnerable to theft. It may be safer to use the money as soon as possible, in paying staff salaries, for example, or buying things for the programme such as fuel. In Boga, Zaire, the cash received as fees for service was used to buy cattle, since there was no bank available to keep money safely. When cash was needed to buy materials or supplies, a cow was sold. Doing this meant that not only was the money kept safely, but by investing it in a saleable commodity, it held its value at a time when rampant inflation was destroying the value of cash holdings.

5.4.3 Supervision and control

It is advisable that responsibility for dealing with any aspect of money is shared, since situations where just one person knows the system are open to abuse. Generally, the more that financial information can be shared openly among members of staff, the better, since this tends to dissolve the basis for rumours and suspicions that can arise around closed or secretive accounting. The people in charge of collecting money, paying for goods and services, and doing the accounts should be regularly supervised and their work cross-checked to pick up on any irregularities. A simple system is again preferable since a complex system provides more room for error and inconsistency.

Staff should be aware of the disciplinary consequences of the misappropriation of funds, from the very beginning. A definite penalty relating to any theft must be recognised, and be enforced, so that a clear message is given. Cases should not be kept secret but be dealt with openly — covering up theft is a dangerous precedent.

These same guidelines apply also to the control of stock, such as fuel, vehicle parts, and particularly drugs, since valuable goods such as these are also vulnerable to misappropriation. A supervisor should regularly check the stock and be able to account for its legitimate use in the records.

5.5 Monitoring and evaluation

In the same way as accounts are monitored, as discussed above, it will be useful to monitor many specific aspects of the programme regularly to see how well plans and targets are turning out in practice. A continuous process of monitoring allows changes and adjustments to be made which facilitate the attainment of objectives. Evaluation is a more formal and much less regular exercise than monitoring. Evaluations tend to look back with a broader view and point to strengths and weaknesses of the programme as a whole.

The receipt and release of stocks and supplies, the quality of care, staff performance and satisfaction — these are aspects of programmes which could be subjects of monitoring and evaluation. The methods used in such exercises are many and could include talking to health workers, clients, and the population at large; looking at records and physical stocks; and simply observing daily activities. Monitoring and evaluation are dependent upon the collection, analysis and use of appropriate information.

The International Network for Rational Use of Drugs (INRUD) has developed a series of indicators to monitor drug use. Prescribing practice and drug management are very important features of many health programmes, and they become especially so if money is being raised through the sale of drugs. Details of the indicators are given in Appendix 5.

6 The rural health zone of Boga, Zaire

This chapter describes the health programme in Boga,[1] and its means of financing. Then the nine questions which were outlined in Chapter 4 are discussed in relation to the situation in Boga. The chapter thus provides an example of the application of these questions to a particular situation. It is hoped that readers will then be able to apply this method to other actual health programmes with which they are concerned.

Case study: Health care in Boga, Zaire
Boga lies in the north-east of Zaire, close to the Ugandan border. The health zone has the smallest population of any in the country — its exclusively rural population of some 25,000 is largely poor and subsistence-based. It is geographically isolated with very poor road access across the zone.

The government of Zaire has, in all its health zones, designated the responsibility for providing health care to specific agents. In Boga it is the Anglican Church which holds this responsibility. The government provides no resources for health care. Instead, these resources are generated principally from the community through charging fees, but the remaining financing comes from the Church Health Services (CHS), external donor agencies, and community contributions. Until recently, almost all the recurrent costs and 20 per cent of capital costs were covered by the community.

A user fee was charged for a consultation and also for subsequent treatment given. Each person paid a fixed fee, which was graded according to age (pre-school infants, school-age children, and adults), for each out-patient consultation at the health centre or hospital. On top of this, each individual paid for all treatments given (drugs, dressings, injections) and all procedures undertaken (laboratory tests, X-rays, surgery). The structure of drug charges was their purchase cost plus 100 per cent. The mark-up of 100 per cent was principally intended to cover transport costs and high taxes (roughly 36 per cent in all) levied on imports. It still meant that the drug charges were competitive with the prices of the private drug sellers. In-patients paid the same treatment costs, plus a standard bed-fee per day.

To give an idea of the cost and relative affordability of health care, the price of certain treatments in 1990 are given below. They are not stated in money terms since prices and exchange rates change so frequently that monetary prices have no meaning.

The cost of treating a five-year old for malaria was equivalent to the price of three eggs or 0.5kg of rice. The cost of treating an adult for malaria was twice that amount.

The cost of treating a five-year old for bronchitis was equivalent to nine eggs or 1.5kg rice.

To put that in the context of earnings in the locality: a watchman could have expected to earn roughly the value of 25 eggs (4kg rice) per week, and a registered nurse roughly 40 eggs (6kg rice). In other words, the treatment for an adult with malaria cost about one quarter of a watchman's, and one sixth of a nurse's weekly wage. A typical family relying on subsistence farming would not have had such good access to cash, and the amount of cash they had would vary according to the season. They would probably only have had as much as the watchman in a very good month just after the harvest.

Patients were charged on the spot and were expected to pay. There was no formal system to allow for credit, but no-one was refused treatment if they had no money with them. In such a case a payment note was issued and followed up later. People were not refused treatment in an emergency if they did not have the money. If they were not able to pay later on, they were allowed to give their labour as payment, or to contribute in kind with produce such as chickens. Exemptions were given for orphans and for leprosy patients. Exemptions on the grounds of poverty were granted on the recommendation of the village development committee (VDC).

Church Health Services were responsible for the fabric of buildings, which were usually maintained through a combination of local support and donations from overseas. Most of the external donor support took the form of one-time grant money covering specific capital requests (such as buying vehicles or extending buildings), but donor money also funded one expatriate staff member. Community contributions of labour and materials supported the construction of buildings and equipment.

The nine questions posed in Chapter 4 will now be answered in respect of Boga.

6.1 What services are provided?

The zonal hospital in Boga has 50 beds, accommodating medical, surgical, paediatric, maternity and intensive-care services, although they are very basic. The out-patient department, which has a simple laboratory, sees about 600 new patients per month.

There are five health centres and four health posts in the zone, which carry out preventive and curative Primary Health Care. One of the health centres is a referral centre, which can accommodate up to 20 in-patients and has facilities for emergency surgery, including Caesarian sections and minor procedures.

In each village there is a village health worker (VHW) who is chosen by the village development committee. The VHWs promote health care in the community and provide routine treatment of common complaints. They carry a small supply of medicines which they sell to patients. They attend monthly meetings for on-going training, to discuss problems and to re-stock their supply of medicines. The VHWs are paid a regular sum, which is provided jointly by the village, the Collectivity (the local council) and the Health Zone.

It is clear that the health care provided in the zone is promotive, preventive and curative. However, it is only the curative care which is charged for and which therefore raises money for the continuation of the services. Has this in some way led to an over-emphasis on curative services in Boga?

Preventive health care in Boga is given the importance it deserves, and there is an uncommonly high immunisation coverage — 95 per cent of children under five are reportedly fully immunised, most of whom have completed their immunisation by the age of 1 year.[2] And promotive health care has not been forgotten even though it is often harder to do. The VHWs promote health care in the villages, for example by encouraging families to build pit-latrines. The community determined that latrine building was a priority health need and so there was tremendous social pressure on families to construct their own. Each village chief also had the authority to fine families who did not have a latrine. As a consequence, almost every household now has a latrine. Village development committees, together with the VHWs, conduct village surveys, looking at such things as water and sanitation. The emphasis given to preventive and promotive care is illustrated by the importance given to VDCs and VHWs. They are seen as integral to Primary Health Care, and evidence of this high regard given to VHWs is the fact that the regular payment of their salaries is shared by three parties and not simply left to the community to bear.

6.2 What incentives are created for user and provider?

The incentive given to encourage people to utilise the preventive health services is the fact that they are free of charge. There is no fee for services such as growth monitoring, immunisations and antenatal check-ups. A further way of encouraging antenatal care is by charging pregnant mothers reduced fees for any treatment needed during the ante- and post-natal period if they book their hospital delivery early on in the pregnancy.

The fact that the patient must pay for every drug makes the patient cautious about demanding a large range of drugs. However, on the part of the health workers there is no particular disincentive to guard against over-prescription, and it has been found that there is much over-prescribing in the zone (over-use of antibiotics and injections). Since each health centre is expected to be self-supporting with regard to its recurrent costs (which include salaries), there is a hidden incentive for the staff to generate as much income as possible. It is suspected that this is manifesting itself in over-prescribing. Monitoring and supervision are not adequate to control over-prescription on a day-to-day basis. In response to this, standard treatment guidelines have been introduced, which it is hoped, along with improved monitoring and supervision, will alleviate the problem.

There are plans to reform the fee system to one whereby patients pay a fixed fee per episode of illness. The reasons for change are many, but among them is the desire to remove the link between drugs prescribed and the fee that is paid. Such a system might cause patient dissatisfaction, since someone prescribed a mild treatment may protest when they witness someone else paying the same amount but receiving more. On the other hand, this system would be much more in keeping with the cultural concept of health as one of 'wholeness', since it would allow the patient to complete the treatment and attend for follow-up without the fear of having to pay again.

6.3 Who uses the services and who pays: is the programme equitable?

The burden of *payment* for health services falls entirely on the sick, since payment is only made for curative care. Generally, since it tends to be the poorer people who are most vulnerable to sickness, it also tends to be the poor who are shouldering the burden of payment. Although the very poorest can be treated free of charge on the authority of their village chief, it is quite often not just the money which is a barrier to their receiving treatment. A common worry is that they do not have suitable clothes to wear to the hospital or health centre and are ashamed to go for that reason.

Exemptions are also made for the chronically sick (e.g. leprosy patients), and there are subsidies to reduce the high cost of drugs for TB patients. This is done by a cross-subsidy where a relatively greater mark-up is made for other less essential drugs (e.g. injectable vitamins), and this money used to subsidise the TB treatments.

The fees raised from those who pay must cover the cost of treatment for those who do not pay for whatever reason. If there are some people who are able to pay but receive free treatment (e.g. health staff), while at the same time there are people who are less able to pay but are required to do so, then there is room for a more equitable distribution of the burden of payment. However, it is currently the law in Zaire that health workers are given the benefit of free treatment as part of the job, so there is no scope to change this practice.

Those who *benefit* from the service are those who have access to it. Access can be interpreted in several ways. Firstly, in a geographical sense: the health centres and health posts are relatively well-dispersed throughout the zone so that physical access to them is not greatly different for anyone. The exception is the hospital, which is convenient for the residents of Boga but is very far away (up to 60 kilometres) for those who live at the other end of the zone. Secondly, in a monetary sense: those who can afford to pay or to borrow the money, or can claim exemption, have access, while those who cannot, do not have access. Thirdly, access is denied to those who are unable to provide in a non-monetary sense. For example, for in-patients it is necessary to have relatives able to provide food for the duration of the stay. This might not be possible for some people, to whom access is thereby denied.

The fees and other factors will inevitably deter some people from using the health services, and they might use traditional healers or drug sellers instead, or alternatively receive no treatment at all. In a recent rapid community survey, 56 per cent of households said that the price of treatment was the greatest obstacle to their receiving medical care. There is, however, no routinely-collected utilisation data to reveal which population groups might be deterred from using the health services.

6.4 Are sufficient resources raised?

Until 1989, roughly 75 per cent of recurrent costs were paid for with money generated from fees paid by the community. In addition, approximately 20 per cent of capital costs have been covered by community contributions. Donor support has made up the rest.

This achievement, to cover such a high percentage of recurrent expenditure exclusively from resources raised in the community, is remarkable and extremely unusual. There are a number of features specific to the programme and the community which have allowed this to be possible. Firstly, careful financial planning and accounting has meant that realistic prices could be charged which were high enough to cover costs, but which were still affordable by most people in the community. All prices were reviewed monthly in an effort to keep them in line with rising costs. Secondly, the quality of service provided has been high enough for people to be willing to use the services and pay for their treatment. Thirdly, and importantly, the salaries paid to health staff are relatively low, which has kept overall costs down. It would seem that health workers' salaries are far lower than equivalent salaries in neighbouring African countries — this is probably an important reason for the high level of cost-recovery which has been achieved.

There are some aspects which have been lacking in the programme because of their high cost. To give one example, supervision of health workers has not been as regular as desired, since the cost of frequent transportation around the zone is very high. Insufficient resources were being raised to cover this expense. This issue is being addressed with the hope of restoring supervision to the important position it deserves. More frequent supervisory visits would be desirable, and would contribute to an improvement in staff morale and better-quality treatment practices. (See 6.6)

The Zairean economy has suffered very badly in recent years and rampant inflation has been persistent. In such a situation cash does not keep its value since prices keep rising, and there is always a concern over what to do with the money collected from patient fees. An innovative scheme existed for a while where the money was used to buy cows, as the price of cattle would stay in line with generally rising prices. When the money was needed to pay salaries or buy supplies, the cash was raised by selling the cattle. This scheme lasted for three years. It ended because there was inadequate care of the cattle, in that they belonged to an institution rather than an individual. The process of buying and selling had also become complicated.

The programme managed its foreign-exchange needs for many years by keeping the foreign currency paid as grants from overseas donors, and using it to buy drugs from abroad. The money raised locally through fees was then used to finance the particular project for which the grant was given. In this way, it avoided the difficulties caused by exchanging money.

The last few years, however, has seen the programme run into financial deficit, for a number of reasons. Extremely rapid devaluation of the currency has raised all prices, and the cost of living, to such an extent that some people can no longer afford the services. Poor management, and severe devaluation continue to be a threat to the programme. (see 6.7)

6.5 Is there much waste and inefficiency?

A WHO-recommended list of essential drugs has been in use for some years. This streamlines the procurement and stocking of drugs which are bought through a non-profit making agency in the UK, selling pharmaceutical supplies at cost price. This works out even cheaper than buying locally-produced drugs. These measures, of course, cannot in themselves ensure appropriate prescribing by the health staff. The use of standard treatment guidelines which guide the health worker in treatment procedures, coupled with regular monitoring of prescribing practices of the kind outlined in Appendix 5, would go some way to improving the efficiency of drug use. Improved supervision could also help here.

It is much more expensive to treat minor cases in hospital than at the health centre. In order to encourage efficient use of the different levels of care, a higher fee is charged at the hospital for treatment of a non-referred (and non-emergency) ailment than is payable at a lower-level facility.

The policy of using locally-made goods as far as possible is intended to minimise the amount of money that is wasted both on transporting goods and in paying higher prices to a chain of traders. The community has made and donated many items of equipment for the hospital, such as sheets, blankets, and operating gowns. Local cotton is used for sutures, and local cough mixtures are prepared. The hospital staff even learned how to make their own intravenous fluids which reduced the need to import them and also pay high import taxes.

The nurses at each facility collect the fee money and record information in registers. Monthly returns are then submitted to the administrator. The Chief Medical Officer checks the money handling once a month, but since the fee structure is complicated, it is not so straightforward to check. It is apparent that better controls are needed because there has been money lost through theft. While it is recognised that theft can not be entirely stopped, it is clearly desirable to minimise it. The accounts are checked by an external auditor once a year.

An important aspect of trying to reduce waste and inefficiency in the system is to monitor the accounts regularly, which is done with care in Boga. In this way it is possible to have an idea of which areas are over-spending and to investigate them further, with the intention of taking action. Annual evaluations also provide helpful information on this aspect of programme management.

6.6 What is the quality of health care provided?

In the past, the quality of health care at Boga has been relatively good, and the community has had confidence in the services provided. This has been evidenced by the utilisation of the health services, and the level of community involvement. Quality of care is, however, one area which has deteriorated of late, both from a medical point of view, and in terms of the quality perceived by the patients.

From the community's and staff's own evaluation of the programme in 1991, it was found that the fabric of some health facilities was very run down and the equipment in a poor state of repair. Patients also complained of the lack of politeness and respect shown them by the staff. The quality of medical care at primary health care level has declined, with the staff displaying poor prescribing practices — giving partial prescriptions and generally using drugs 'irrationally'. For example, while standard treatment guidelines were brought into use, it was found that staff rarely had printed copies available to them to work with.

These things taken together contribute to the significant problem of very poor staff morale. Staff are paid extremely low salaries, endure poor living conditions, and professionally feel isolated and unsupported because of the inadequate supervision they receive. Improvements in the quality of care are being sought through addressing the issue of staff support in general, and particularly the issue of supervision. A significant change which is being investigated is to see if staff salaries can be financed from another source, rather than relying on patient fees to generate income for salaries. If an alternative could be found, the salary would be paid irrespective of the patient load at each health facility.

6.7 Is the programme sustainable?

The history of the health programme since its establishment as the Boga Comprehensive Health Care Project in 1981 has some bearing on the issue of its sustainability. It has always been very much a community-determined programme, where the community has had ownership of it and a strong commitment to it. The community first identified its own needs and priorities, and the health programme was set up to address some of these.

At this time, the community was acutely aware of the need for self-reliance and of the dangers of creating something that it could not sustain itself. There has always been an awareness of the need to set only realistic aims. The principle of cost-recovery was not established as an objective in itself, but as a means of achieving a sustainable health programme. Thus, the sociological context of the health programme with its roots in the culture of the community has contributed much to its sustainability.

For over ten years the programme has been almost completely self-reliant, depending only on a small amount of donor input for mainly capital projects. It has been well-managed and flexibly run which has improved the chances of its sustainability. There are a number of factors which mitigate against its sustainability in the longer term. One factor is the small population size — with a population of only 25,000 it is the smallest health zone in the country.[3] The health programme is reliant on people continuing to be willing and able to pay, and any change in this situation (even amongst a small proportion of the population) is likely to have a significant impact on the programme. Because of its relatively small population, Boga is likely to be more vulnerable to this change than other zones.

A second factor is a much larger problem, which is currently affecting the whole country. The sustainability of the health programme is seriously threatened by national economic insecurity. Successive, rapid devaluations of the local currency have dramatically raised the cost of imports, and this has had a knock-on effect on prices in general. To give an example, the value of the Zaire against the US dollar in August 1991 was 15 times less than its value had been, under a year previously, in November 1990. High taxes on goods compound this, as does inflation; and in an environment of economic crisis it is difficult to know whether or how sufficient resources will be generated to maintain the health programme as it has been, in Boga. During this period of uncertainty, it seems likely that support from external donors will play a greater role.

6.8 Are local people involved in planning and managing the health services?

The health programme in Boga, from its inception, has been a community-determined programme. It arose as a response to the identification by the community, of the need for health care. In 1987, the community defined 'health', surveyed local health needs, and established priorities and strategies. In 1991 the community made its own evaluation of the programme. Health workers at all levels, administrators and managers are from the community, but it is felt that there could be more direct involvement by the community in daily management issues.

6.9 What is the impact on other health care providers?

The Zairean health system makes the Chief Medical Officer responsible for **all** health activities in the zone. In the rural health zone of Boga, this means that a Catholic and a Brethren Health Centre also come under Boga's supervision. All the centres work closely together.

The only other possible providers of health care are the traditional practitioners or private drug-traders. No recent attempts have been made to collaborate with the traditional healers and they function quite independently of the health programme. They do not see the Boga programme as a threat, but instead have given their ideas on how they think the programme could be made more accessible to the community.

Although the price of a full course of drugs at health centres is lower than the private drug-traders charge, it is possible for people to buy partial treatments (one or two tablets at a time, or possibly a single injection) from the drug-trader. Many people prefer to do this, since they can obtain at least some drugs, for a lower outlay. Currently, private drug-traders are flourishing in the area. They are easily accessible to people, and they are getting more business from patients who are finding it increasingly difficult to afford more than a small amount of money at a time. The possible impact of this behaviour on health is a concern for those involved in the health programme.

6.10 Conclusion

As we said in the Preface to this book, our aim in presenting the material has been to stimulate thinking and provide guidance on the issue of financing health care. The strategy we have adopted here has been to provide some discussion of the relevant issues through presentation of illustrative examples. These reflect experiences that people have actually faced in tackling those issues.

As an appropriate closing note, we would like to emphasise the fact that there are no 'right answers', and therefore no neat prescriptions for financing and running a health programme. Problems will be solved, and new problems will arise. While we have not presented any magic solutions, it is nevertheless hoped that readers have found this book informative, and that it will be of practical support to them in their varied endeavours.

Appendix 1: The Bamako Initiative

The Bamako Initiative — so called, because it was first announced at a meeting of African Ministers of Health held in Bamako, Mali, in 1987 — is an initiative jointly sponsored by WHO and UNICEF. It arose in response to the economic crises facing many countries of sub-Saharan Africa, and the concern that the deteriorating economic situation was having an adverse impact on health and health programmes. The sustainability of many PHC programmes was being threatened by restricted health budgets and the reluctance of donors to continue to fund recurrent programme costs.

The Initiative proposed generating revenue through community-financing, by charging fees for essential drugs. Both drugs and revenue would be made continuously available by creating a revolving drugs fund. The revenue from the drug sales would be used to buy new supplies of drugs, which again would be sold. The revolving drugs fund was to be managed at community level, with the hope of specifically addressing the issue of sustainability.

Furthermore, it was hoped that the sale of drugs could subsidise the provision of other health services which had little or no income-earning potential. If a substantial mark-up over and above the drug costs was allowed for when price-setting, a surplus would be generated which could be used to finance aspects of PHC. A particular emphasis was given to supporting mother-and-child-health activities in this way.

UNICEF, in conjunction with other international agencies such as the World Bank and the African Development Bank, were to provide initial drug supplies and support costs for a limited time (three to five years), after which it was hoped that the revolving drug funds would have become sufficiently well-established to continue independently.

The Initiative aroused considerable debate amongst development workers involved in PHC, academics, and non-governmental organisations with experience in community financing. Criticism was levelled at different aspects of the Initiative: the model of PHC portrayed in the Initiative was naïve, simplistic, and 'vertical' in approach; it did not pay sufficient attention to the managerial and operational problems encountered in community drug sales; the ambitions for cost-recovery were unrealistically high; its assumptions were based selectively on the experience of a few small-scale projects, ignoring conflicting evidence from other similar projects; that successes from small-scale projects could not necessarily be generalised when implementation was expanded into national programmes; and that it shifts the major costs of Primary Health Care from the governments to consumers. The other major concern was the serious problem of the pharmaceutical industry's flooding of the African countries with unnecessary and irrational medicines in the face of foreign-exchange shortages.

In subsequent years, the guidelines on the implementation of the Initiative have evolved and been adapted to specific country circumstances. A variety of cost-recovery mechanisms have been adopted, apart from direct payment for drugs, including payment per episode of illness, and pre-payment schemes. The Bamako Initiative now manifests itself as a variety of different things. 'It seems that, as long as the three components of community financing, community participation, and essential drugs are covered, the Bamako Initiative can be taken to mean almost anything relating to strengthening basic health services.' (Kanji, N. 1992)

Below, are three references on the Bamako Initiative, one early and two recent:

WHO (1988) *Guidelines for the implementation of the Bamako Initiative,* WHO Regional Committee for Africa.

Jarrett, S and Ofosu-Amaah, S (1992) 'Strengthening health services for MCH in Africa: the first four years of the Bamako Initiative', *Health Policy and Planning,* 7; 2, pp. 164-176.

Kanji, N et al (1992) *Drugs policy in developing countries*, Zed Books. Chapter by Hardon and Kanji 'New horizons in the 1990s'.

Appendix 2: Household surveys and baseline information

When deciding what form of health financing to adopt, and what prices to charge, you should find out what the local community already pays for health care and what it thinks about the various forms of finance.

One possible method is to conduct a household survey. Ask questions about:

- The types of health care which people use (traditional practitioners, drug shops etc).

- How much people spend on health care (cash or in kind). This should include 'extras' such as the cost of transport.

- Where the money used for health care came from. Was it already in the household? Was it borrowed? A gift? Did something have to be sold in order to raise money for health care? (Remember that seasonal factors may be relevant here).

Do not ask questions about the distant past — people cannot generally remember details of minor illnesses that happened more than two weeks previously.

If you want to ask people about their *opinions*, it is better to hold a group discussion. Groups could discuss questions such as:

- Who are the poor people in the community? Should they pay for health care?

- Would insurance work in the community?

- What should the structure of fees be?

For further information on household surveys, see Nichols, P (1991), and the book by Kielmann A et al. (1991). Focus group discussions are used in Waddington C and Enyimayew K A (1989) and (1990). Full references can be found in Bibliography and Further Reading.

Appendix 3: Threats to the sustainability of revolving drug funds

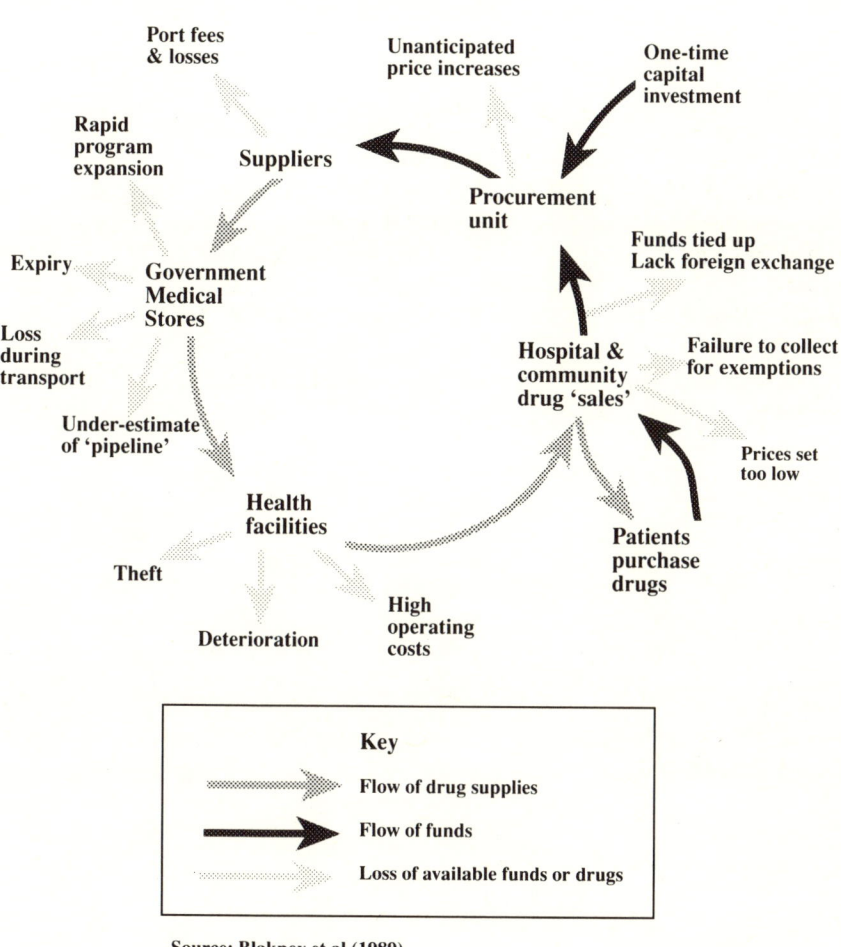

Port fees & losses

Unanticipated price increases

One-time capital investment

Rapid program expansion

Suppliers

Procurement unit

Expiry

Government Medical Stores

Funds tied up
Lack foreign exchange

Loss during transport

Failure to collect for exemptions

Under-estimate of 'pipeline'

Hospital & community drug 'sales'

Prices set too low

Health facilities

Theft

Patients purchase drugs

Deterioration

High operating costs

Key

Flow of drug supplies

Flow of funds

Loss of available funds or drugs

Source: Blakney et al (1989)

Appendix 4: Suppliers of low-cost drugs and equipment

ECHO and IDA supply low-cost drugs and equipment to not-for-profit organisations.

ECHO
(Equipment to Charity Hospitals Overseas)
Ullswater Crescent
Coulsdon
Surrey CR5 2HR
United Kingdom
Telephone: 081 660 2220
Telex: 924507 ECHO G
Fax: 081 668 0751

IDA
(International Dispensary Association)
PO Box 3098
1003 AB Amsterdam
The Netherlands
Telephone: +31 2903 3051
Telex 13566 IDA NL
Fax: +31 2903 1854

Appendix 5: Steps towards rational prescribing and appropriate use of drugs

1 Standard treatment guidelines

Drugs are very often used inappropriately and inefficiently. Standard treatment guidelines provide clear information for health workers, specifying appropriate treatments for a whole range of different diagnoses. They support the use of essential drugs and can help to reduce the amount of unnecessary drug use by improving prescribing patterns.

Standard treatment guidelines cannot of themselves improve prescribing practices — it is clear that they must be put into use in order to have an effect. Regular supervision of the health workers will show if the guidelines are being followed, and monitoring the prescribing practices will confirm this.

2 Monitoring drug use

The International Network for the Rational Use of Drugs (INRUD) has developed a series of indicators which can be used to monitor drug use. The 13 indicators are listed on the next page. They can be used for four main purposes:

- describing drug-use patterns
- monitoring and supervisory activities
- making comparisons between areas or over time
- evaluating the impact of interventions

INRUD also publishes a free newsletter called *INRUD News*, and supplies Lotus 1-2-3 spreadsheets for data collection in drug use surveys. INRUD can be contacted at Management Sciences for Health, 165, Allandale Road, Boston, Massachusetts 02130, USA. Fax: (617) 524-2825.

Also useful for keeping up-to-date on aspects of drug management is the *Essential Drugs Monitor*. This is available free from Essential Drugs Monitor, World Health Organisation (WHO), 1211 Geneva, Switzerland.

INRUD indicators

Indicators of prescribing practices

1 Number of drugs prescribed per patient encounter.
2 Percentage of encounters during which an antibiotic is prescribed.
3 Percentage of encounters receiving one or more injections.
4 Percentage of encounters treated in accordance with national or local standard treatments for up to five important tracer conditions.*
5 Percentage of drugs prescribed in generic form.
6 Percentage of drugs prescribed not included on the national essential drug list or local formulary.

Indicators of adequate patient care

7 Average patient consultation time with a prescriber.
8 Average time spent by patient with a pharmacist or dispenser.
9 Percentage of patients who receive an examination meeting minimum criteria for adequacy for up to five important tracer conditions.
10 Percentage of patients able to report the correct dosing schedule for the self-administered drugs they receive.

Indicators of drug information and availability

11 Percentage of prescribed drugs actually dispensed at the health facility.
12 Percentage of health facilities where a national essential drug list is available.
13 Percentage of key drugs for treating five important tracer conditions available in health facility stores.

* Tracer conditions refer to selected key conditions or diseases which it would be important to follow up.

Appendix 6: Sample budget

Recurrent items

	Local currency shillings	Foreign currency $
Personnel		
2 Senior health workers	300	
3 health workers	300	
Administrator	80	
Driver	60	
Vehicle		
Running and maintenance*	600	
Supplies		
Medical	100	525
Non-medical	100	
Buildings		
Utilities (elec/water)	40	
Maintenance	20	
2 Training workshops**	118	

Capital items

Equipment		
Refrigerator	75	
Sub-total	1,793	525
10% contingency	179	53
TOTAL	1,972	578

Budget notes

* Estimated 100km/month @ p0.5/km.

** 3-day workshop with 1 external facilitator, 5 participants:

Facilitator's per diem	24
Workshop materials/stationery	20
Food	15
	59

Appendix 7: Setting prices

First, decide which system of fees you want to use: cost plus mark-up; fixed fee per treatment; fixed fee per episode of illness. (These were outlined in Chapter 3). Then follow the steps for whichever you decide on. Any estimates made of numbers (e.g. prescriptions, new attenders etc.) could be based on past records. For new programmes, a guess will have to be made, which can be adjusted as monitoring information becomes available.

1 Cost plus mark-up — price closely reflects the actual cost of drugs prescribed.

This pricing method sets individual drug prices which closely reflect the actual cost of the drugs. This would mean that a patient would pay more for a relatively expensive drug, such as an antibiotic, than for a cheap drug such as acetylsalicylic acid (aspirin).

Step 1
Decide what the total cost you want to recover is.

This may be the purchase price of the drugs, plus transportation, plus import duties, or may also include some other costs such as a contribution towards salaries. You decide.

Worked example: Say you aim to recover 1,000 shillings, 800 of which represents the full purchase and transportation cost of one consignment of drugs for three months. You aim to raise 200 shillings for fuel for the vehicle this quarter.

Step 2
Estimate what percentage mark-up over the cost of drugs you will need to charge in order to recover that amount of money.

You will need to account for anticipated losses here (losses incurred due to drug wastage, money handling errors, theft, etc.).

Worked example: If there are no losses, you already aim to recover 200 shillings on top of the cost of drugs. This already represents a mark-up of 25 per cent on the cost. You estimate that an additional 2.5 per cent of the total cost of drugs should cover reasonable loss. (2.5% of 800 = 20.) So, taking the cost-recovery aim and the estimated losses into account, the mark-up on the cost of drugs needs to be (25% + 2.5%) = 27.5%

Step 3
Estimate the number of prescriptions that will be exempt from the fee.

Worked example: It is estimated that 15 per cent of prescriptions will be exempt from the fee. Assuming that these will be average-priced prescriptions, this represents 15 per cent of the total cost of drugs, or (15% of 800) = 120 shillings.* So, taking the cost-recovery aim, the estimated losses and the exemptions into account:

The mark-up on the cost of the drugs needs to be (25% + 2.5% + 15%) = 42.5%.

Step 4
Calculate the cost price of each drug item prescribed, and add 42.5 per cent.

Clearly, doing this for each different drug item can be a time-consuming and complicated task. Alternatively, you could calculate the cost of an average adult prescription for a specific diagnosis, say, malaria, and add 42.5 per cent. This still involves much complexity, and leaves plenty of room for errors to be made, both in the calculation and in the collection of fees and their checking. For this reason alone, it is simpler to charge a fixed fee for treatment, rather than cost plus mark-up (see 2 below).

Step 5
Confirm from your information from the community that people would be willing and able to pay this fee!

2 Fixed fee for treatment — fixed fee for each prescription or each prescription item.
Follow **Steps 1 and 2** above.

Step 3
Estimate the number of prescriptions that will be exempt from the fee.

Worked example: It is estimated that 15 per cent of prescriptions will be exempt from the fee. (This information is used in Step 4).

Step 4
Calculate the price of each prescription (or each drug item). Do this by **dividing the total cost plus the mark-up** which accounts for the cost-recovery

---

* If the prescriptions being exempted turn out to be more expensive than average, or if there are more exemptions given than you estimated, then you will be *underestimating* the value of drugs given through exemptions. If on the other hand, the prescriptions being exempted turn out to be cheaper than average, or there are fewer exemptions given than average, then you will be *overestimating* the value of drugs given through exemptions.

aim and anticipated losses (end of Step 2), **by the estimated number of prescriptions (or drug items) which will be paid for**.

Worked example: Total cost of drugs + 27.5% Mark-up = 800 + (27.5% of 800)

$$= 800 + 220$$
$$= 1,020$$

If the estimated number of prescriptions in the next three months is 4,800, then the number of prescriptions which will be paid for is 4,800 - (15% of 4,800) = 4,080. Therefore the price to set is 1,020 ÷ 4,080 = 0.25 shillings per prescription.

If the estimated number of drug items given in the next three months is 12,000, then the number of drug items which will be paid for (assuming an average of 2.5 drug items per prescription) will be 12,000 - (15% of 12,000) = 10,200. Therefore the price to set is 1,020 ÷ 10,200 = 0.1 shillings per drug item.

This raises the price to patients of relatively cheap treatments. You may want to reduce this somewhat by creating a few different price bands according to simple criteria, such as the nature of the prescription, whether it includes an antibiotic or not, diagnostic groups, etc.

Step 5
Confirm from your information from the community that people would be willing and able to pay this fee!

3 Fixed fee per episode of ilness
Follow **Steps 1 and 2** as above.

Step 3
Estimate how many episodes of illness will be exempt from payment.

Worked example: It is estimated that 15 per cent of illness episodes will be exempt. (This information is used in Step 4).

Step 4
Calculate the fee per episode Do this by **dividing the cost plus mark-up** (at the end of Step 2) **by the estimated number of illness episodes which will be paid for**.

Worked example: The estimate of episodes of illness is equivalent to numbers of new cases seen. If this is estimated to be 3,200 in the next three months, then the number of episodes which will be paid for is 3,200 - (15% of 3,200) = 2,720. Therefore the price to set is 1,020 ÷ 2,720 = 0.375 or, rounded up to a convenient figure, 0.4 shillings per episode of illness.

Step 5
Confirm from your information from the community that people would be willing and able to pay this fee!

Appendix 8: Examples of Cash Book Records

Receipts				Payments			
Date	Details	Receipt number	Amount	Date	Details	Receipt number	Amount
8 March	Cash in hand		2500.00	10 March	Phone/fax	1	150.00
10 March	Donor grant	211	6589.00	15 March	Office stationery	2	300.00
14 March	Course fees	212	3500.00	2 April	Purchase of medical supplies	3	700.00
				4 April	Vehicle fuel	4	20.00
4 April	**Total**		**12589.00**	**4 April**			**1170.00**

Balance (4 April)
11419.00

Example of a cash book with receipts and payments shown separately

Analysed cash book payments

Date	Details	Receipt number	Amount	Personnel	Supplies	Travel	Vehicle running & maintenance	Equipment running & maintenance	Commun-ication	Other
10 March	Phone/Fax	1	150.00						150.00	
15March	Office stationery	2	300.00		300.00					
2 April	Purchase of medical supplies	3	700.00		700.00					
4 April	Vehicle fuel	4	20.00				20.00			
Total			1170.00		1000.00		20.00		150.00	

Appendix 9: Inputs for a health programme

Costs	
Recurrent	**Capital**
Personnel *Supervisors, health workers, administrators, technicians, consultants, casual labour*	**Vehicles** *Bicycles, motorbikes, 4-wheel drive vehicles, trucks*
Supplies *Medical supplies: drugs, vaccines, dressings.* *Office supplies: stationery.* *Teaching supplies: flip charts, posters*	**Equipment** *Refrigerators, sterilisers, scales, furniture, cool boxes, clinical implements*
Travel costs *Train, bus, airfares, travel allowances*	**Buildings (construction or purchase)** *Health centres, hospitals, training centres, offices, storage facilities*
Building running and maintenance *Rent, electricity, water, heat, cleaning, repairs, insurance*	
Vehicle running and maintenance *Gasoline, diesel, lubricants tyres,spare parts, registration, insurance*	
Equipment running and maintenance *Maintenance, spare parts*	
Communications *Telephone, telex, fax, postage*	
Other	

Bibliography and further reading

Abel-Smith, B (1992) 'Health insurance in developing countries: lessons from experience', *Health Policy and Planning*, 7;3, pp. 215-226.

Blakney, R, Litvack, J and Quick, J (1989) 'Financing primary health care: experiences in pharmaceutical cost recovery', Arlington, V A, *Management Sciences for Health*, PRITECH Project, HSS-035-IR.
An excellent compilation of country experiences in pharmaceutical cost-recovery. Draws together the lessons. Available free of charge from Management Sciences for Health, 1925, North Lynn Street, Suite 400, Arlington, Virginia 22209, USA.

Cammack, J (1992) *Basic Accounting for Small Groups*, Oxford: Oxfam.
An excellent beginner's guide to accounting.

Chabot, J, Boal, M, Da Silva, A (1991) 'National community health insurance at village level: the case from Guinea Bissau', *Health Policy and Planning* 6;1, pp. 46-54.

Christian Medical Commission (undated) *Financing Primary Health Care Programmes: Can they be self-sufficient?*, Geneva: World Council of Churches.
From a CMC study on financing church-related community-based primary health care. Available from CMC, World Council of Churches, 150, Route de Ferney, 1211, Geneva, Switzerland.

Clark, J with Davies, M (1991) *A simple guide to structural adjustment*, Oxford: Oxfam.

Creese, A (1990) *User Charges in Health Care: A review of recent experience*, Strengthening of Health Services Current Concerns Series 1, Geneva: World Health Organisation.

Creese, A and Parker, D (1991) *Cost analysis in primary health care: a training manual for programme managers*, WHO/Aga Khan Foundation /UNICEF
A detailed and practical description of how to calculate health service costs. Available from The Publications Office, World Health Organization, 1211 Geneva 27, Switzerland.

de Ferranti, D (1985) 'Paying for health services in developing countries: a call for realism', *World Health Forum* 6, pp. 99-105.

This article is a short version of an influential paper by de Ferranti (1985) *Paying for Health Services in Developing Countries: An overview*, World Bank Staff Working Paper 721, Washington DC.

* Gilson, L (1988) *Government Health Care Charges: Is equity being abandoned? A discussion paper,* EPC Publication 15.

Grandin, B E (1988) *Wealth Ranking in Smallholder Communities: A field manual*, London: Intermediate Technology Publications.

Available from Intermediate Technology Publications, ITDG, 103/105 Southampton Row, London WC1B 4HH.

*Hoare, G and Mills, A (1986) *Paying for the Health Sector: A review and annotated bibliography of the literature on developing countries*, EPC Publication 12.

Jarrett, S and Ofosu-Amaah, S (1992) 'Strengthening health services for MCH in Africa: the first four years of the Bamako Initiative', *Health Policy and Planning* 7;2, pp. 164-176.

Kanji, N, Hardon, A, Harnmeijer, J M, Mamdani, M, and Walt, G (1992) *Drugs policy in developing countries*, London: Zed Books.

Kielmann, A, Janovsky, K and Annett, H (1991) *Assessing District Health Needs, Services and Systems*, AMREF/GTZ.

Describes how to conduct household surveys and to find out more about the services offered at health facilities themselves. Available from AMREF, Wilson Airport, PO Box 30125, Nairobi, Kenya.

* Mamdani, M and Walker, G (1985) *Essential Drugs and Developing Countries: A review and selected annotated bibliography*, EPC Publication 8.

Mandl, P (1988) *Annotated Bibliography on Community Financing for Local Health Services*, UNICEF Staff Working Paper 3.

Millard, E (1987) *Financial management of a small handicraft business*, Oxford: Oxfam.

This is a simple book about financial management of a small business. It can help to separate out basic business ideas from considerations that are specific to the health sector. It is more useful than many accounting textbooks, which are unnecessarily detailed.

Nichols, P (1991) *Social Survey Methods: A guide for development workers*, Oxford: Oxfam.

Nickson, P (1991) *'Evaluation and auto-evaluation of the rural health zone of Boga'*, unpublished report.

Save the Children Fund (UK) (1990) Seminar on the sustainability of health services, Wadham College, Oxford, 3-6 July 1990. Case study presented by Peter Thompson.

Save the Children Fund (UK) (1992) *'Financial constraints to sustainable health sector development in Nepal'*, Draft unpublished report.

Stinson, W *et al.* (1987) *Community Financing of Primary Health Care: the PRICOR Experience — A comparative analysis,* PRICOR, Maryland.

Waddington, C and Enyimayew, K (1989) 'A price to pay: The impact of user charges in Ashanti-Akim District, Ghana', *International Journal of Health Planning and Management,* 4, pp. 17-47.

Waddington, C and Enyimayew, K (1990) 'A price to pay: The impact of user charges in the Volta region of Ghana', *International Journal of Health Planning and Management,* 5, pp. 287-312.
These articles consider the impact of an increase in government health service fees in Ghana. Assessment methods used include focus group discussions.

Waddington, C (1992) *'Health economics in an irrational world: the view from a Regional Health Administration in Ghana'*, unpublished PhD thesis, Liverpool University.

Walt, G (ed) (1990) *Community Health Workers in National Programmes — Just Another Pair of Hands?* Milton Keynes: Open University Press.
A comprehensive discussion of community health workers, including a chapter by Lucy Gilson entitled 'Sustaining community health worker programmes: who pays?'

Wamai, G (1991) *'Community health financing in Uganda — Kasangati Health Centre cost-recovery programme: a two-year report 1988-1990'*, unpublished report.

World Bank (1987) *Financing Health Services in Developing Countries: An agenda for reform,* A World Bank Policy Study, Washington: World Bank.

World Health Organisation (1988) *Guidelines for the Implementation of the Bamako Initiative,* Geneva: WHO Regional Committee for Africa.

Young, H (1990) *The Use of Wealth Ranking in Nutrition Surveys in Sudan,* RRA Notes 8, IIED Sustainable Agriculture Programme.

---

* These are publications from the former Evaluation and Planning Centre for Health Care, and are available from the London School of Hygiene and Tropical Medicine, Keppel Street, London WC1E 7HT.

Notes

Chapter 1

1 The declaration made at the WHO/UNICEF-sponsored International Conference on Primary Health Care, held in Alma Ata in 1978. It drew up the fundamental principles of Primary Health Care to which most national governments subsequently gave their signatures of commitment.

2 In 1985, de Ferranti estimated that the world-wide resource shortage for meeting the targets of primary health care was $50 billion per year.

3 World Bank (1987) *Financing Health Services in Developing Countries: An agenda for reform*, Washington: World Bank.

Chapter 2

1 The information about BELACD was kindly provided by Bernard François.

2 Tables 1 and 2 give figures in percentages because we are interested in the relative shares provided by different sources of finance. It is difficult to attach a meaning to actual monetary amounts, because of the problems of translating the real value of various currencies over time.

3 Christian Medical Commission (undated), *Financing Primary Health Care Programmes: Can they be self-sufficient?*, CMC: Geneva.

Chapter 3

1 The material for this example was taken from an unpublished report: Wamai, G (1991), 'Community health-financing in Uganda - Kasangati Health Centre cost-recovery programme: a two-year report, 1988-1990'.

2 The material for this example was taken from Chabot, J et al (1991) 'National community health insurance at village level: the case from Guinea Bissau', *Health Policy and Planning* 4:1, pp.46-54.

3 Walt, G (1991), *Community Health Workers in National Programmes: Just Another Pair of Hands?* Milton Keynes: Open University Press.

4 Abel-Smith, B (1992), 'Health insurance in developing countries: lessons from experience', *Health Policy and Planning* 7:3, pp. 215-226.

5   Save the Children Fund (UK), (1992), 'Financial constraints to sustainable health sector development in Nepal', draft unpublished report.

Chapter 4

1   The authors would be interested to hear of any examples.
2   Equal expenditure per capita, equal access for equal need, equal utilisation for equal need — these are examples of differing definitions of the equity goal. See Gilson, L (1988) *Government health Care Charges: Is Equity Being Abandoned?* A discussion paper EPC Publication, 15.
3   ibid
4   Waddington, C (1992), 'Health economics in an irrational world: the view from a Regional Health Administration in Ghana'. Unpublished PhD thesis, Liverpool University.
5   This information was kindly gathered and supplied by Sue Chowdhury.
6   For a published reference on similar material see Waddington C and Enyimayew, K (1989) and (1990),'A price to pay...' Parts 1 and 2, *International Journal of Health Planning and Management* 4 (1989) and 5 (1990).
7   See Grandin, B E (1988) *Wealth Ranking in Smallholder Communities: A Field Manual*, London: Intermediate Technology Publications; and Helen Young (1990) 'The use of wealth ranking in nutrition surveys in Sudan' in *RRA Notes* 8, IIED Sustainable Agriculture Programme, London: IIED.
8   See Blakney R et al, (1989), *Financing Primary Health Care: Experiences in pharmaceutical cost recovery*, Arlington, V A, Management Sciences for Health, PRITECH Project, HSS-035-IR.
9   Creese, A (1990), 'User charges in health care: a review of recent experience', *Strengthening of Health Services Current Concerns Series 1*, Geneva: WHO.
10 Blakney R et al, op. cit.
11 ibid.
12 Sustainability in the health sector is:
    • 'the survival of health projects and programmes after an initial period of investment' (Development Assistance Committee, OECD)
    • 'the ability of a health programme to deliver services or sustain benefits after major technical, managerial and financial support from a donor has ceased' (USAID)
    • 'the capacity of the health system to function effectively over time with a minimum of external input' (Save the Children Fund).
13 Save the Children Fund (1990), Seminar on the sustainability of health services, Wadham college, Oxford, 3-6 July 1990. Case study presented by Peter Thompson.

Chapter 5

1 See also Cammack, J (1992) *Basic Accounting for Small Groups*, Oxford: Oxfam.
2 Personal communication, Jarl Chabot.

Chapter 6

1 The information for this case study was gathered by our colleagues Pat Nickson and Nyangoma Kabande.
2 Nickson, P (1991) 'Evaluation and auto-evaluation of the rural health zone of Boga'. Unpublished report.
3 When the health zones were established in 1982, government reckoning was that each zone would require a population of between 50,000-100,000 in order to be financially self-sufficient.

Index

Abota 15, 36, 37
Absenteeism 34
Accountability 43
Accounts 43
Alma Ata, Declaration of 2
Antenatal care 22, 39
Antibiotics 24
Bamako Initiative 3, 58
Bank account, 46
Baseline information 7
BELACD 8
Bilateral aid 20
Boga, Zaire 48
Book-keeping 43
Budget 39
  notes on 42
Capital costs 41, 48, viii
Capital expenditure viii, 41
Capital goods 10
Cash 6
Chad 8
Chloroquine 22, 32
Church Health Services 49
Church-run programmes 29
Clinics 29
  mobile 22
Colonial administration 2
Community 6, 28, 56
  health 2
  involvement 37
  loan scheme 28
  participation 21, 59
Community health worker 14, 17, 22
Contingency allowance 41
Cost recovery viii, 3, 30, 58
Cost-recovery potential 32
Cost sharing viii
Costs 6, 8, 28
  hidden 9
Cross-subsidisation ix, 13, 22

Curative services 11, 13, 22, 50
Current balance 43
Demotivation 16
Debt 2
Declaration of Alma Ata 2
Dentists 23
Devaluation ix, x, 30, 42, 55
Diarrhoea 22
Donor agencies 16, 36
Drugs
  selection of 30
Economic crises 2
Efficiency 21
Equity 21, 24
Essential drugs ix, 58, 63
Essential drugs list ix, 24, 33
Estimates 39, 40
Evaluation 47, 54
Exemptions ix, 13, 27-29, 49, 51
  of health staff 28
  treatment-based 27
Expenditure
  budgeted 33
Family planning 10
Fee
  fixed per visit 23
  flst 24
  per episode 12, 14, 24, 51, 68
  user 23
Fees 3, 4, 29, 30, 35, 42
Fixed fee 12, 48
Foreign exchange 2, 41, 53
  shortage of 59
Free markets 3
Fundraising 18
  community 7
Gastro-enteritis 24
Generic drugs ix, 33
Ghana 25, 29
Gonoshastya Kendra 26

Government financing 18
Government health services 29, 38
Grants 16
Group discussion 60
Guinea Bissau 7, 15, 24, 31, 32, 36, 37
Healers
traditional 7, 30, 38
Health care
national context 6
private 3
Health insurance scheme 7
Health services provision 24
Health services
evolution of 2
Health-services delivery 1
Hospitals, mission 2
Household economy 7
Household survey 7, 25, 60
IMF ix, 3
Immunisation 9, 29, 39, 50
Incentive payments 14, 34-35
Incentive
financial 31
Incentives 23, 31, 35, 50
negative 23
positive 23
Income generation 17
Indonesia 3, 10
Inefficiency 32, 54
Inflation ix, 30, 40, 46, 53
annual rate of 40
Inputs 6
INRUD 47, 63
Insurance 14, 42
International Monetary Fund ix, 3
International Network for Rational Use of Drugs
47, 63
Kagando, 22
Kasangati Health Centre 13, 22
Kasangati 24, 28, 30, 32, 33, 35-36
Khartoum 38
Latrines 22
Malaria 32
Mark-up ix, 12, 48, 58, 66
Monetarism x, 3
Money
control of 45
handling of 45, 54
Monitoring 21, 29, 32-34, 35, 44, 47, 51

Morale 14, 34
Mother-and-child-health 58
Multilateral donor 20
Nepal 20
NGOs x, 8, 10, 38
Nigeria, 35
Non-governmental organisation x
Objectives 21
Official development assistance 20
Operating costs x
Oral rehydration solution 24
Over-prescribing 24, 51
Participation 37
Payment in kind x, 27
Pit-latrines 50
Planned expenditure 39
Pre-payment schemes 14, 24, 31, 35, 59
Prescribing 22, 24, 32, 33, 35, 47, 63 ·
Preventive services x, 12, 13, 22, 50
Primary Health Care x, 8, 9, 22, 24, 25, 33, 58
Priorities 6, 29, 56
Private drug-traders 30, 38, 56
Private health-care 3
Private sector 3, 4
Privatisation 3
Promotive x, 11, 22, 50
Public health
measures 2
risks 27
Quality of health car 1, 34, 54
Quality of patient care 14
Quality of service 52
Reaganism 3
Receipts 43, 45
Records 45
Recovery potential 30
Recurrent costs x, 31, 41, 48
Recurrent expenditure x, 52
Revolving drug fund x, 36, 38, 44, 58
Salaries 55
expatriate 9
Savings clubs 28
Service delivery 1, 34
Service quality 21
Social insurance 19
Social security 19
Socio-economic status 26
South America 19
Stabilisation, economic 3

Standard treatment guidelines   xi, 24, 33, 35, 51, 53, 54, 63, xi
Stock control   47
Structural adjustment   3, x, xi
Sub-Saharan Africa   2
Subsidies
  hidden   29
Subsistence economy   6
Supervision   9, 33, 34, 35, 39, 46, 51, 53, 63
Survey
  household   25
Sustainability   10, 21, 29, 36, 38, 55, 58
Taxation.   18
TB   10, 27, 51
TBAs   10, 39
Thatcherism   3
Tontine   28
Traditional birth attendants   10, 39

Traditional healers   2, 7, 30, 38, 52, 56
Tuberculosis   10, 27, 51
Uganda   1, 13, 22
UK   23
UNICEF   58
United States   1
User fees   11, 23, 26, 48
Utilisation   25, 35
Vaccination   22
Vaccines   8
Village health worker   15, 24, 50
Volta   25, 29
Voluntary work   16
Waste   32, 54
Willingness to pay)   30
World Bank   xi, 3, 20, 58, xi
Zaire   46

Oxfam Practical Health Guides

No.1   **Selective Feeding Programmes**
        Dr Tim Lusty and Pat Diskett

No. 2   **Refugee Health Care**
        Dr Paul Shears and Dr Tim Lusty

No. 3   **Implementing Multiple Drug Therapy for Leprosy**
        Dr A. Colin MacDougall

No. 4   **Tuberculosis Control Programmes in Developing Countries**
        Dr Paul Shears

No. 5   **Controlling Iodine Deficiency Disorders in Developing Countries**
        Dr David Phillips

No. 6   **Registration in Emergencies**
        John Mitchell and Hugo Slim

No. 7   **Food Scarcity and Famine: Assessment and Response**
        Helen Young